PURPOSE: LIVE IT!

"FROM A BLANK MIND TO A PURPOSE FILLED LIFE"

TO Alejandro!
You are the Bomb!
As you embark on this
new chapter, may you do it
with purpose! Remember
our chats in class and be
all you were made to be!
I love you
&
God Bless!

GODZCHILD PUBLICATIONS

Published by Godzchild Publications
a division of Godzchild, Inc.
22 Halleck St., Newark, NJ 07104
www.godzchildproductions.net

Printed in the United States of America 2012— First Edition
Cover Design by Tito Garcia
Titogarcia82@gmail.com

Library of Congress Cataloging-in-Publications Data
Purpose: Live It! - From A Blank Mind To A Purpose Filled Life/Eliana Reyes

ISBN 978-1-937095-42-0 (pbk.)

1. Reyes, Eliana. M. 2. Purpose 3. Spiritual Growth 4. Christianity

Table of Contents

To my Lord, Savior, and lover of my soul, Jesus Christ.:
I am eternally indebted to you. Thank you for fully living out your purpose, and for giving me an opportunity to do the same.

To you:
who desire a better and more purposeful life.

To My Readers

You are a weapon of mass construction. In you is the ability to create, the ability to believe, the ability to love, and the ability to be. What you are holding in your hands can be very powerful if you choose to use it. We often think that knowledge is power, but actually, the application of knowledge combined with a pure intention can be very powerful. I'm sure you have questions about your purpose. You may know what it is, or simply need instructions on how to live it out. The focus of this book is to show you that you are full of purpose. Therefore, knowing and understanding why you're on earth will catapult you into living with purpose, on purpose. If you're not living for something greater than yourself, then what is the point of living?

You may be sitting in a classroom right now, or on your daily shift at work feeling unsatisfied about life. You might be in a church or given a new title at work and yet, you feel no direction. If you have reached the point of frustration and you are tired of the "same ole same ole" and crave a deeper knowledge of who you are, then this book is for you. Read it with an open mind. If you could only take one thing that I will share with you and use it, you have already moved a step up in life.

Much of what I've learned about purpose and life is captured in this book. Of course, I am still living and discovering lessons about this journey. I don't claim to be an expert, but rather a valuable contributor to your understanding about life, worth, and purpose. The intention of this book is to show you that the discovery of purpose is a process. My goal is to add to your understanding so that you are inspired to deliberately seek your purpose until you find it and live it out.

Why I Wrote This Book

Growing up, I had questions. I was curious about life, God, myself, and purpose. My goal in life was to be a good daughter and student so the idea of having a purpose was never a reality to me. Even though I was not aware that I was seeking it, purpose was happening all around me. It was in college, however, that I realized that the reason I live is purpose! It's the glue that keeps me together. Purpose is like an inward propeller that wants to drive the greatness out of us, the one ingredient that should be present in every aspect of our lives! It was also during college that I developed a relationship with Jesus Christ. This spiritual bond led to the incredible discovery of my purpose, but also to the realization that living with purpose first requires a process, one that I am still on!

I wrote this book for two reasons: it was part of MY purposeful process to do so and because I want to see YOU ALIVE to purpose!

How To Use This Book

The book has a total of nine chapters and they are broken down into three sections. The first section focuses on knowing purpose. This happens when we do three things:

1) know what purpose is and what it is not,
2) get intimate with the Giver of our purpose
3) take inventory of our gifts (which are the tools given to us to accomplish that purpose).

The second section focuses on understanding purpose. We understand our purpose through our relationships (bad and good), our daily issues, and the hardships we experience that build our character. Both knowledge and understanding will make your life's purpose worthwhile. How to live out your purpose and how to discover the different arenas to do so, is covered in the third section of the book.

For the sake of clarity, I have attached a glossary to identify some of the words I use constantly. You can find those at the end of the book under the "purposeful extras" section. Take a look at them before starting the book. I make a distinction between purpose, calling, gifts, and intentions amongst other words. As well, throughout the book, I will use a few quotes from the Bible. There are three main versions: New King James Version (NKJV), New International Version (NIV), and The Message (MSG). At the end of the quote I will indicate which version it is for your study purposes.

In addition, at the end of each chapter you will see some reflection questions. Please take the time to fill out those questions. Think about them. Write about them. Talk about them. As you meditate on them I promise you, clarity will become your best friend. Some thoughts in this book may not apply to you. Take what does, and run with it. For those of you who want to apply what you've learned immediately, you will notice a "Live It" tip at the end of the reflection questions.

If you skim through this book you will get some powerful nuggets that will influence your thinking.

If you read through it and reflect on what I'm saying you will get some understanding of where YOU are.

But if you believe the words written, allow yourself to feel the heart in which it was written and take it a step further by writing or even sharing what you are learning with someone,

I promise you that the revelations you will receive will change your life.

WHAT'S IN IT FOR YOU?

My desire is for you to know, understand, and come to a place of loving the fact that you have a mission in life so that you can live it everyday. I want you to have clarity and a new perspective on the popular topic of purpose. You have a reason of being in this world and it matters to God and to those around you.

And by the way, I'm not here to twist your arm about religion or God. I am not a fan of "religion." I am a woman passionate about my relationship with God and madly obsessed with seeing people wake up to their God-given purpose! I am only presenting to you my thoughts and a part of my life for the sake of growth and understanding to your life. At the end of the day, believing, changing or becoming motivated to seek your purpose in God is up to you.

I pray this book serves as a tool of reference, confirmation, encouragement and even enlightenment to your life, as you discover why you were made to live—why not purposely?

Introduction

Once upon eternity, the most wonderful book was written. It was the most beautiful story you will ever read. It was a story of love, sorrow, mystery, trials, and even destiny. But when read carefully, from beginning to end, it revealed an interesting secret. One that can only be understood by the author Himself, and by the main character: YOU. That's right; our Creator wrote the story of our lives before we were even created. As He sat on his throne with his might and splendor and looked into planet Earth, He realized that something was missing. "How can I make my dream come true?" He thought. Suddenly, the most creative idea came to mind. He thought of you! Immediately He took out his special box. In it were millions of gifts, talents, characteristics, and qualities that He would place in you. After much thought, He took out the ones He would give you and carefully wove them into your being. Everything was nearly perfect, but there was one vital element missing. He selected His "secret box," opened it, and thought again about his dream. Gladly, He removed the "special substance" and placed it in you. He called it PURPOSE, the fuel to your life; it's the reason the story of you was created in the first *place. Finally, He was ready to send you to Earth, and with one breath... it began.*

Two days before the 2012 New Year, I sat at Dunkin Doughnuts all night doing some final edits on the manuscript. After meeting with a good friend who expected to receive my final draft by midnight, I felt an urgency to just sit down and finish! The fact that I had no motivation to work on the book for 2 weeks, gave me some extra motivation at the moment. I was very excited to just go with the flow. It was 7 p.m. I had my headphones on so that I could focus. *The power of focus and commitment is amazing!* All night, I noticed a gentleman sitting at the table in front of me. He stared at me with intense focus. Every so often he would smile. I thought to myself: "is this one of God's angel encouraging me to keep going?" It was a silly question but this man was purposely looking at me.

Four hours passed.

I was so full of energy and purpose that I simply could not stop writing. I felt purpose was coming out of my pores. There was no way I was going to meet the midnight deadline. So I asked for more time and continued to "flow." The man was still there. He was not working on anything in particular neither was he drinking coffee. Why was he staring at me? His look was very genuine.

At 2 a.m., I finally removed my headphones to relax for a bit. Immediately, the man spoke to me in Spanish and asked:

"What are you working on?" I told him I was just writing. Persistently he asked: "But what are you writing?" So I told him that it was a book. The minute I said "a book," his eyes lit up! He stood up as if he was waiting for me to say that. Suddenly he said: "A book?! I wrote a book too, want me to show you?"

Without waiting for my answer, the gentleman grabbed a chair, sat next to me, and showed me his handwritten stuff. At that moment it hit me: "I'm in the middle of a divine purpose appointment with this stranger! The flow in me is not for me, but to help this man with his gift of writing!" Immediately, I saw his work in its first stages of the vision. He confessed that he was discouraged with the project. He shared some of his financial and technical difficulties which had hindered him from writing. Lastly, he shared his desire to settle pending business in this country so that he could go back to Dominican Republic to be with his family (he had not seen them for 2 years). He then confessed why he had been staring at me all night. He said he was in admiration of me and he didn't know why. I told him that he must have been admiring God in me. With a sly giggle, he told me, "You are like God to me. You have His form."

At that moment, I received a revelation of what was happening.

Here is a man God has inspired to write a book, but the daily trials of life were hindering him. It made sense that God made me pregnant with purpose, and it was that purpose that motivated a man with the same gift to finish what he started. After finishing our conversation I had to laugh. I had just experienced the same thing that I was writing about. That is the essence of purpose. Purpose is something we must live everyday, and when we realize we are pregnant with purpose, the very essence of God, it inspires others to wake up to theirs.

Part One

Know Purpose

KNOW PURPOSE

"My people are destroyed for lack of knowledge..." Hosea 4:6 NKJV

In this section, you will learn the importance of knowing purpose. You can't " Do YOU " unless you KNOW you. This section focuses on knowing three particular things in order for you to know your purpose:

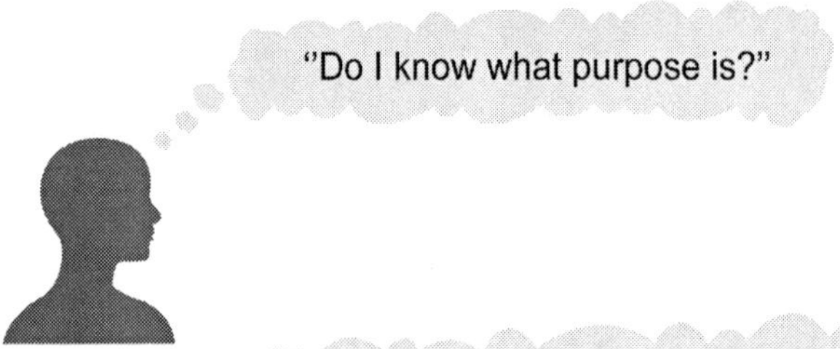

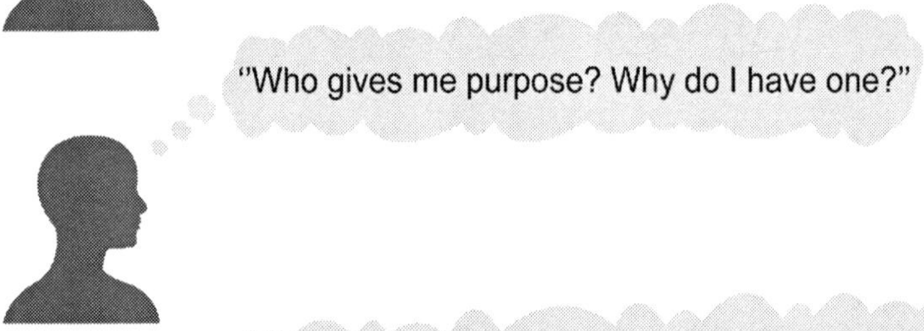

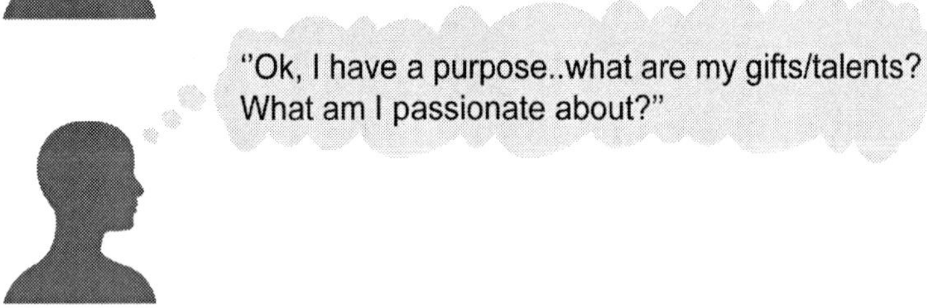

CHAPTER 1: PURPOSE RE-DEFINED

"And we know that in all things God works for the good of those who love him, who[a] have been called according to his purpose" Romans 8:28 (NIV)

At some point in life, we have all asked ourselves the same questions: What is my purpose? Why am I alive? What am I supposed to do on earth?

These were the questions that ran through my head during high school. Quite honestly, I never pursued purpose because I never knew I had one. High school years were masked by temporary pleasures and vanities. The reality was that I was seeking for something bigger to eliminate the emptiness and worthlessness I felt inside. Everyday lacked direction. My daily goal was to do well in school and enjoy life. I thought that being a good girl and being obedient to "rules" was my life's mission. Despite the fact that I had no idea what I was supposed to do, I knew I was created to do great things. There was more to life and I wanted to find it.

College seemed to be the most logical answer. I thought like many of you probably did at some point, "My purpose will be found in some type of career. If I find where I fit in, then I will be happy. If I go to the right school, everything will be good. If I find the right job..." I used my college years to find that one career that would solve all of my problems and bring me joy, but soon I discovered that I had multiple talents and interests that did not really fit in one place. College prepares you for a career, not a purposeful calling. Immediately I had to find another method.

Sometimes looking for outward answers will frustrate our inner solutions.

The truth is, we all search for purpose at some point in our life. The ways we search may vary, but the end result (clarity on who we are and what we are supposed to do) is what we desire. If you do a quick Google search on the topic of purpose you will see that much is already written on the topic. In fact, as you go through each of the links, it can be a little overwhelming to read the same "lingo" on every page (e.g., discover your purpose, birth the new you, find yourself, etc..). I remember the countless times I did this trying to see if there was one good article, one piece of advice that would tell me what my purpose was so that I could obey it. My focus was more on doing than on simply being. Sometimes looking for outward answers will frustrate our inner solutions.

Therefore, the first step of living out your purpose is to KNOW what it is and what it isn't. It's not a matter of whether or not you have a purpose, you do. It's not a matter of discovering or finding it. It's a matter of understanding what is in you and what has been entrusted to you. This happens as you LIVE.

You can't DO you unless you KNOW you. So, let's define it.

Purpose is why something is done, why something is created, or why something exists. Purpose is also the function or role of something. Purpose is the WHY you are who you are and the reason you are here on earth.

You can't DO you unless you KNOW you.

Everything has a purpose. The chair you are sitting on, the car you drive, the clothes you wear, the perfume you have on, and even the book in your hand. People have a purpose. Animals have a purpose. God has a purpose, many purposes in fact. We are all "pregnant" with a seed of purpose. This means that everything that has been placed in us has a function. To understand this definition, you first have to believe that you were created with a purpose. You did not just appear randomly in this world. You did not come from a monkey. You are not the residue of a big explosion. You did not come from a Fairy Godmother who waved her wand and chanted you into existence. No! You did not just come to be on your own, OUT of nothing, FROM nothing, FOR nothing. Once you understand that you were created, the next logical thought is that there must be a Creator that must have had a reason to create you. We will discuss that in the next chapter.

For now, there are four things that I want you to know about purpose:

1) purpose is out-of-the-box,
2) purpose is an action statement,
3) purpose in you is a solution to a societal problem
4) purpose is multi-dimensional.

PURPOSE IS OUT-OF-THE-BOX

Most of us are trained to think inside of the "box." We are born inside of a box called family and from there we are passed on from box to box. As a young Hispanic woman who grew up in a city area, I was trained to think inside of the "box." What's inside of the box?

Tradition, expectations, one way of doing things, living like everyone else, self-imposed theologies, and the "system" are some of the many things inside of this "box." For example, my family defines success as having a college degree, landing a good job, and being a professional in your field. So you can imagine the pressure when I was in college! I needed to meet that standard! I was letting outside forces define what was IN me, instead of letting what was IN me define the outside. Society measures success based on money, fame, glory, and accomplishments. But all that fades with time. An everlasting success is measured by the fulfillment of your purpose and what was produced as a result of it.

Unlike what society coins as "successful," our purpose is outside of the box. It's unexpected. You can't contain it. You can't understand it sometimes. It surprises you even when you know it. Your purpose is bigger than a major. Your purpose is larger than the career you choose. Your purpose is greater than your own life!

It's so easy to get caught up in thinking inside of a box. I have spoken to so many students who all share the same concern I did, "what am I supposed to do with my life?" Even after graduation there is a sense of misdirection. Why? Because everyone is putting pressure on you to have your life figured out by a certain time! The problem with that is that you are more than a box, so you will always have the struggle of wanting to fit in somewhere. We get frustrated when we try to put ourselves in the right box and can't find it. It happens in school, the business world, family and even church! If we can just find the right boyfriend, girlfriend, career, church, etc.... If we can only find the right box we belong in, then our life would be perfect. Right? FALSE.

Do you remember being in elementary school? If you do, I'm sure you will agree that everything in Kindergarten up until the third grade revolved around one thing: crayons! Every one had a box of crayons. Crayons were like our daily bread! They made things easy. They were diverse and fun to look at. They were so useful when it came to coloring and creativity. Our purpose is like crayons. It's meant to be brought out of the box and used up completely, just like in elementary school. Though there may be shades of the same color, every color is still unique. Your purpose is the same, unique to you and out of the box.

So instead of being contained in a box, pretending to be someone you are not, and listening to what everyone else says about you, think of yourself as a person full of life. There is a crayon called purpose in your hand. Hence, coloring is a life long enjoyment.

Get the picture? How can you color if you are still in the box? Now ... if you just finished reading that and you feel mad because you already have a college degree and still feel "in the box," don't worry! Nothing you have under your belt will go to waste. Trust me. Focus on what's ahead. It's NEVER too late to get outside of the BOX! Here is another tip, don't let people pressure you into thinking that you have to have life "all figured out" now. Life is a journey! Everyone colors a different page.

In chapter 3, we will talk more about the "colors" or talents you have in your hands. Once you figure that out, it's just a matter of putting it to use!

PURPOSE IS AN ACTION STATEMENT

Now once you realize purpose is out-of-the-box, the second thing to know is that purpose is an action statement.

Let me share a revelation that helped me. Purpose is not a vocation or an occupation. Purpose is the engine that drives you, the personal mission that gives meaning to your vocation or occupation. This means you are constantly doing it and walking it out regardless of the occupation or field you are in. Living with purpose becomes automatic once you know what it is.

Oftentimes we are so limited in our thoughts of purpose. I tend to ask many individuals "what is your purpose?" the most typical answers I get are:

"My purpose is to be a teacher."
"My purpose is to be a doctor."
"My purpose is to own a business."
"My purpose is to be a good person"
"I don't know. Maybe help people in some way."

While these are all great things, they are not your purpose. Hence a person can't say "my purpose is to be a Math teacher." They may be functioning in the role of a math teacher but that is only a vehicle for what they are meant to do. Teaching may be their gift, but it doesn't equate to their life's purpose.

Think of the example I gave you in the last section. I said

our purpose is out-of-the-box like crayons. Think of the purpose of a crayon (to color). It would be silly for a crayon to say, "My purpose is to BE RED." Rather, its purpose is to COLOR RED. If a crayon tells itself: "I need to be red" it can do that inside of the box with NO ACTION happening. But saying, "I need to color red," will automatically propel the crayon to fill in the blanks it encounters, with its rich color. *See the difference?*

Another example comes from one of my favorite characters in the Bible, Paul, the apostle. Paul was one of these passionate, aggressive, "ride or die" kind of dudes. He was an extremist; all or nothing. Prior to being a Christian, he was a radical murderer of Christians. He hated them so much that he killed many and was constantly persecuting them. Little did he know that his purpose was wrapped around his greatest hate. The Bible says in Romans 1:1 (NKJV), "Paul, a bondservant of Jesus Christ, called to be an apostle, separated to the gospel of God." This makes one thing very clear. Paul was first and foremost a servant of Christ and his occupation was to be an apostle. The role of an apostle is to start churches and set things in order. However, if you continue reading his story his purpose becomes very clear:

"to produce obedience in the Gentile people based on faith in Jesus Christ."

Read that again. His purpose was "to produce obedience based on faith in Jesus Christ." It's an action. Regardless of the church he went to or where he preached, the apostle Paul would teach with hopes that the people would obey and change their ways. The many letters he wrote, the way he taught, and his constant desire to set order in the churches, were all venues or platforms to accomplish his main purpose. We will talk about platforms in the last chapter of the book, for now just remember that purpose is an action statement.

PURPOSE IS A SOLUTION

Now that you know that purpose is out-of-the-box and always in constant action, the next thing to know is why? Purpose is a solution to a societal problem. There are countless societal problems (e.g. poverty, hunger, depression, abuse, sickness, etc). People seek answers! The answer can be a powerful word, a loving embrace, or a sense of hope. The answer can be you. If the purpose in you is a solution, then finding the problem is priority. Let's think about this.

We live in a world where everything we need is a click away. Thus, getting from one place to the next is easy. I know it's hard to imagine but once upon a time cars were nonexistent. People walked to their destination or maybe got on a horse. Traveling consumed most of their time and soon the desire to shorten that time became a priority. How else would they make the most out of the day? Consequently, people were faced with the problem of not arriving to a set location as fast as they hoped. Eventually someone saw this dilemma and invented the automobile. While there are many contributors to the automobile, the purpose of it remained the same to this day: to transport from point A to point B. It doesn't matter if cars today are used for a different reason (e.g. taxi cab, limos for weddings, races, etc...) or if they come in all different shapes, sizes, and even colors. Their purpose still remains.

The same is true for us. We were created to solve a problem in life. Whatever that problem is, we are equipped to handle it. This explains why there are certain causes that grab our attention more than others. Or why certain issues break our heart more than others. For example, I always gravitate towards the fatherless, especially young women who lack a father figure. Dysfunctional relationships and the hopeless also tug at my heart. So, I have learned that part of the problem I am meant to solve in life is in those areas.

PURPOSE IS MULTI-DIMENSIONAL

I was having a conversation one day with a young lady who confessed how confused she was when it came to purpose. She said, "I don't know what my purpose is but I know I have many. I just don't know how to identify all of them." Although I understood exactly what she meant, I did not have the words to make her understand it at the moment. Let's go back to the example from the last segment. Cars have the same basic purpose (to transport from point A to point B). However, because cars differ in color, shape, and model, their "second" or "outer" purpose is different. There are race-cars, taxi cabs, limos, trucks, luxury cars, and cars that carry mail! Similar to cars, we have the same inner purpose: to serve God (someone greater than us) and one another, but because we differ in talents, stories and callings our outer purpose will vary. Deep down inside, we all have the desire to help or serve people. The difference will be in how, where, and with what we do. That's what you need to find.

So, let us be clear here. We were all created with the same inner purpose. We all have a different "HOW" to manual to satisfy that inner purpose. In addition, as we live in the direction of our purpose, we may have "temporary" purposes that help us get better prepared for what we are supposed to do in life.

Now that we have established what purpose is and is not, it's time to answer the next question: *how do I start knowing my purpose? Where do I stand right now on that journey?*

PURPOSE REFLECTION

1. What are some of the pressures that keep you thinking and living "inside of the box?" Is it family expectations, traditions, self-imposed ambitions?

2. What are the things you love to do as hobbies or passions?
I LOVE TO:

3. What causes or issues have always grabbed your attention? What problem do you think you are here to solve? (check all that apply)

___ World hunger
___ Homelessness
___ Addiction
___ the abused: (mentally, physically, spiritually, or emotionally.)
___ the abandoned
___ those taken advantage of or manipulated
___ The defenseless
___ The helpless
___ The fatherless
___ Widows

___ Elderly

___ Young women

___ Young men

___ The intellectuals

___ The rich

___ The poor

___ Other: ________________________

LIVE IT TIP!

Take one of the things you love to do from question 2 and put it into action! Write down how you will put it into action. (e.g. I love to encourage others and I will put that to use by encouraging someone everyday even if it's myself.)

CHAPTER 2: WHO'S YOUR DADDY?

"... every thing got started in Him and finds its purpose in Him." Colossians 1:16 (MSG)

We have all heard the expression: *"Who's Your Daddy?"* It's a slang phrase people use to really inquire: Who is in charge of you or who is your boss? The phrase itself probably has different meanings to different groups of people, but the intention of this chapter is not to explore that. Before we talk about purpose and before we talk about changing the world, we all need to ask ourselves this question: Who is my Daddy? In other words, who am I living to please?

You see, when we are young, we aspire to be "Daddy's little girl" or "Daddy's" little man. It is our natural desire to make our parents proud. They own us and teach us the way to live (most of them at least). Somewhere along life however, we lose focus and we forget who we are living for. We give ownership rights to boyfriends, girlfriends, and other things. Sometimes, multiple things control us.

Why is this problematic?

Because if we are not clear with the root intention of why we do the things we do, it is impossible to live a purpose-FULL life without reaching destruction. You do not have the power to keep a person continually pleased with your life. People change and so do emotions. Therefore, when I ask, "Who is your Daddy," I am not asking about your biological parents. Some of you may feel anger when thinking of your father, while others may feel delighted because they had a positive upbringing. My intention is not to magnify either feeling.

Instead, I would like for you to consider your Heavenly father. Some of you know Him and some of you don't. However, it makes sense to ask our Creator what we were made for. If you buy a TV and want to know how to use it, you read the manual that was written by the inventor. If you want to know how your new phone works, you read the manual written by the inventor. It's the most common thing to do. In like matter, if we need direction about our purpose, the right person who can tell us is God. After all, we are His invention. Of course we can live life by pushing many wrong "buttons" before we get to the right one. But why waste your precious time? Consider this perspective.

YOU ARE AN INVENTION

Every invented thing in life has an inventor behind it. And every invention has a function or purpose. If we are great inventions of God, then that must mean God had a reason why He created us. The hard part is done (we were created and our life is designed). We now need to intentionally fulfill that purpose so that the world can benefit from it. Your purpose becomes obvious when you know God.

Think about the many inventions in the world and their various functions. Every invention was made as a solution to a problem, as discussed in the previous chapter.

- Stamps were invented by Rowland Hill to make prepayment of mail postage easy.
- Scotch Tape was invented by Richard Drew as a solution to the auto painters' dilemma: their inability to make clean dividing lines on two-color paint jobs.
- Automatic doors were invented by Dee Horton and Lew Hewitt as a solution to the problem of the high winds in Corpus Christi and its damaging effects on regular doors.
- Baby carriages were invented by William Kent to prevent full rotation of a babies body by providing some of the movement and support.
- Band-Aids were invented by Earle Dickson as a result of his wife cutting her finger in the kitchen. Its purpose was to protect small wounds better.
- Chapstick was invented by Dr. Charles Brown Fleet as a solution to chapped lips.
- Cotton swabs or "Q-tips" were invented by Leo Gerstenzang after seeing his wife use cotton and a toothpick to get wax out of her ear.

If all of these nonliving objects were invented with a purpose by an inventor, certainly as humans the same applies. The difference between us and objects is that we are alive. This means that we are living and breathing 3-dimensional people. We are a spirit. We have a soul. We live in a body. If we were just a body with no soul and spirit, we would vanish upon our death. It is our spirit that makes us alive. Once it is gone, only a lifeless body is left. That is what we see in a casket. What is my point? Our purpose is more than what our physical body can achieve. Keep that in mind as you read.

Now every inventor knows that there is no perfect invention. There will always be malfunctions to what is made. Imagine how many drawings artists have to draw before getting that one perfect animation. Even when they get the desired result, from a larger perspective only they know what they originally envisioned and how that particular painting falls short of it. God, who created us knows the same is true for us. He does not hate you. He is not mad at you. He does not expect you to be perfect. The only thing He desires is to have a relationship with you. Why? So that He can impregnate you with His purposes and you can live an abundant life, one that reflects Him. God's perfection can be more easily seen in the life of imperfect people. We are all imperfect, like dirty clay waiting to be formed into something.

GET INTIMATE!

An intimate relationship is the first thing you need in order to walk this path with knowledge and on purpose. Truth is, most people are not living their life's purpose because they are disconnected from their Creator and HIS purpose for their existence. Understanding your life's purpose necessarily means connecting to the intended reasons why God made you in the first place. If you have not found that relationship, seek it and you shall find it through intimacy.

Intimacy is "into-me-you-see" or 'Into-Me-See.' It is an invitation for someone to see into you. Intimacy means you open yourself up and allow someone else to see a part of you that is normally hidden. Intimacy is not only physical (which I'm sure is what first comes to mind when you think of the word). Intimacy can be mental, like when you have a deep conversation with someone. Intimacy can be nonverbal, like when you spend quality time with someone. Intimacy is also spiritual, like when you pray to God or with someone else. Regardless of how you do it, one thing is certain: through intimacy, you get to know someone at a completely different level. It's not superficial.

It is difficult to try to picture this intimacy with God. Is it possible to be intimate with someone we can't see, feel or touch? Absolutely! Being intimate with God means spending time learning about who He is. When we do this we rise up in love for Him and experience his goodness. Remember we are spiritual beings having a human experience so being intimate with God is like nothing you have experienced. It exceeds any natural or self-made "high" you can experience. Why? Because you have limitations as a human being. Intimacy with God satisfies more than your body, it satisfies your spirit and soul. It is in those moments of intimacy that purpose begins to make sense in your life.

There are a few things that happen when you are intimate with God:

- You KNOW your Creator
- You learn who you are
- Your purpose is activated
- You get pregnant with purpose, gifts, and other treasures over and over.

KNOW YOUR CREATOR!

The first thing intimacy does is give you the opportunity to know your Creator. Think about times when you have experienced intimacy (whether physical, emotional, or mental) with someone else. You get to know them more, right? Right. Well, the same is true for God. When you spend time with God, you learn about His character, His personalities and His way of thinking. Outside of God, our purpose does not make sense. Knowing God is the highest accomplishment we can attain. Look at it this way, if we were characters of a Disney movie, knowing Mr. Walt

Disney himself would be a great privilege. He is the person who drew us! The same applies for us. You may be thinking that it's hard to achieve this because we live in a generation that loves information! We want to know everything about everything and everybody! But for what? Do we want to know in order to help others or do we want to know because we want to impress others? If you are going to get knowledge about anything, let it be God. Remember the saying, "it's not WHAT you know but WHO you know?"

LEARN WHO YOU ARE!

As you learn more about God, you start to learn more about yourself. Knowing who you are is a direct result of knowing who God is. This is more powerful than any degree or title you could ever acquire. It is this specific knowledge that opens doors in your life. You start to get revelation of why you are the way you are. You begin to understand your personality, mannerisms, the way you think and even habits. Again, knowledge alone does not mean anything. Ever wonder how is it possible for people to live without purpose? There are many people who are sleeping in their purpose. Days are meaningless, and time passes slowly as they drown themselves in empty thoughts of nothing. Most people don't know what to do in life. Even if they have knowledge or vague ideas about their purpose, without revelation it's void.

Revelation comes during intimacy. What is revelation? Revelation is when you realize something you never did before and your mind is suddenly awakened to that truth. It's what most will call an epiphany or a "V-8" moment. For example, if a 5 year old knows that the refrigerator is full of food but they have no revelation on how to open it, then they won't enjoy the food that's inside. Once they get a revelation from the parents on how it's opened, then their knowledge becomes valuable. Think about the many things you know. How much revelation is connected to what you know?

ACTIVATE YOUR PURPOSE!

The third thing intimacy does is activate your purpose. People are not fulfilling their purpose because they don't know what it is. They have no knowledge of it and are unable to perceive it. Knowledge of your purpose is important because it determines every decision you make similar to a woman who is expecting a baby. There are many decisions that parents can't make until they have the KNOWLEDGE of the child's gender. Once they know its gender, they can select a name, colors for decorations, and they can buy the proper clothing. They begin to prepare. The same holds true for us. Once we are in an intimate relationship with Jesus Christ and we come into the knowledge of our purpose in Him, we then have to prepare ourselves for the next steps. Your life starts when you KNOW your purpose and walk in it.

Pregnant with Purpose

Lastly, during intimacy you get pregnant with purpose, gifts, assignments, and other treasures. Things are birthed in a moment of intimacy. Things like revelation, joy, patience, courage, faith, love, truth and even worth. You may get inspired to write a poem, sing a song, plan an event or even run with an idea. Inspiration happens! You might suddenly be filled with the desire to go feed the homeless or spend time with someone in need of encouragement. This is all wonderful, but in order for them to be "birthed" you need to continually chill with God. Stay in that intimate place! He is not looking for one night stands with you. He is looking for a relationship where He can continually fill you with His purpose. In this relationship, He gives you daily assignments that get you closer to your purpose. If I have a business, I am not going to trust just anyone from the streets to carry out certain tasks. Would you? I am sure Donald Trump and Oprah wouldn't either. Surely, a few tasks could be done by strangers who you hire for less. But those crucial tasks that only people on the inside can do require a relationship and commitment to that business. Some-

He is not looking for one night stands with you. He is looking for a relationship where He can continually fill you with His purpose.

one who can be trusted and is in partnership with them will be entrusted with the task. A businessman's final thought is: "How much profit will that bring in?" Same is true with us and God. We are his business partners, and remember it's HIS business.

> *"Abide in Me, and I in you. As the branch cannot bear fruit of itself, unless it abides in the vine, neither can you, unless you abide in Me. I am the vine, you are the branches. He who abides in Me, and I in him, bears much fruit; for without Me you can do nothing. If anyone does not abide in Me, he is cast out as a branch and is withered...."* John 15:4-6 (NKJV)

Wow. I remember the first time I read this in the Bible. It made me feel so humble inside because at that time I was trying to do things MY way. Like a farmer trying to grow fruit with no seeds, I was trying to produce certain realities in my life by myself. I had to admit to myself that I am nothing but a branch and if I wanted to produce great things in life, then I had to be connected to the right stuff. This quote is telling us something very simple: God wants us to chill with Him. God wants us to be in Him so that He can inspire us to produce things that will empower others to want to do the same: chill with God. When you chill with God, you get inspired to do things you never thought you could do. When you chill with God, you get ideas that no one else has, and you are so motivated that it makes others want to do the same. Certainly, you still have talents and can attempt to have purpose without God. But they will be just that; a talent, an ability, or a career. There will be no evidence of worthwhile "fruit." No fruit.

Are you ready to be a business partner with God? Do you understand that everything you are and all that you have is really His? We are to take care of what has been given to us: talents, relationships, abilities, and our purpose.

Find ways to be intimate with God. At the end of the chapter I have provided different ideas and steps on how you can start to experience that intimacy. You might have been rejected by people, family, church, and loved ones, but just know that God wants you. In fact, He desires intimacy with you. Try it.

BIGGER THAN LIFE

I remember reading a quote somewhere that captured my attention so much. It was stated by Mark Elfstrand. "A man's/woman's purpose is fulfilled when he/she finds something bigger and better than himself/herself to which to offer up his/her life." When all is said and done in your life, a daunting reality sets in: it was never about you. Life is not about you or me, it's about building towards something that's bigger than us and will outlive us.

I am a huge fan of animated movies. Anyone can tell you that about me. It is so easy for me to grasp meaning out of them. One of my favorite animated movies is Dr. Seuss' "Horton Hears a Who."

In that movie we meet an elephant named Horton whose

life got interrupted by a sound. He hears a sound in the middle of his day and lo and behold it was coming from a dust speck that came off of a flower. To his surprise he discovered that there was an entire community named Who-Ville, living in the speck. Little by little he builds a relationship with the mayor of Whoville, and it is because of that relationship that Whoville is saved from destruction towards the end. Watch the movie.

There are 2 key lessons to grasp from this movie. First, the world is bigger than what we think. Second, always keep the big picture in mind. If Horton and the mayor would have never met and formed a relationship, Whoville would've been a non existent, purpose-less place. The same is for us. We live in this world, but in the eyes of God we are like a small community that lives in a dust speck. Our connection with him adds purpose to our lives. All of what you do in life should be a result of your relationship with the Creator. There is a much greater world out there. Live for more.

Our connection with him adds purpose to our lives. All of what you do in life should be a result of your relationship with the Creator.

THE PURPOSE OF PURPOSE

You might be asking yourself, why would God even give us a purpose? What's the purpose of purpose?

The Bible says in Revelations 4:11 (NIV): "You are worthy, our Lord and God, to receive glory and honor and power, for you created all things, and by your will they were created and have their being."

This means we exist because of God. He put the "be" in human BEing since the beginning when he said, "Let there be light." The reason why purpose is given is to advance a greater agenda that will bring others to God. How we go about doing that is what varies, but our goal is the same.

Walt Disney still gets "glory" or fame every time Disney comes out with a new movie. If a dead man is still getting props for something invented decades ago, how much more should a spiritual God get credit for his spiritual inventions that will outlast every earthly creation?

The reality is that most seek purpose but not with a true intention to live it for God. You see, unless God is in the equation, nothing you do will really matter. You can have a career, but without God, it's just a career. You can have that relationship but without God it will just be a relationship. There will be nothing supernatural or outstanding about it, nothing that will outlive you. We don't have the power and magnitude that God has. Therefore we limit our satisfaction and ourselves when we don't let God be the Big Man in our lives.

It's like we are part of an entire orchestra. Some of us are gifted with a voice to sing. Others are gifted with the keen eye and authority to direct. Others have the hands that can play the flute or the piano or even the sax. Regardless of where we stand in this orchestra, we all contribute to the perfect harmony that is created through our unity. In this example, if the purpose of the orchestra is to produce a sound that will bring satisfaction to the listener, then your gift is whatever instrument is in your hand for you to play. And every great orchestra has a director. That is God. If you don't KNOW Him first, how can you know His flow? How can you even be allowed to play your instrument in that orchestra? You choose who you want to play music for. The key is to KNOW the Director, know where you stand and know what has been put in your hand for you to do what you do.

> ...we limit our satisfaction and ourselves when we don't let God be the Big Man in our lives.

PURPOSE REFLECTION

1. Based off what you learned about inventions, what do you think you were invented for? _______________ was invented by God: (your name)

___ to teach ____________________________________
___ to create ____________________________________
___ to build ____________________________________
___ to help ____________________________________
___ to prepare ____________________________________
___ other? ____________________________________

Final statement: ________________________________

____

(e.g. Eliana was created by God to communicate God's purpose, love, and truth to others.)

2. Identify the ways that you can be intimate with God

___ Fasting
___ Practicing silence

___ Praying/ prayer walks or jogs with Him
___ Reading His word
___ Spending time with others who know how to be intimate with Him
___ Dancing for Him
___ Singing for Him
___ Playing an instrument for Him
___ Writing/ Journaling
___ Bible Study
___ Other

3. What are things that you would like to KNOW about your Creator? What are things you would like Him to tell you about yourself?

4. What are the things that stop you from chilling with God?

LIVE IT TIP!

Pick one of the circled activities in question 2 and chill with God today. Ask Him questions and listen. Keep Him in mind as you do.

CHAPTER 3: WHAT'S IN MY PURPOSE GIFT BAG?

"Every good and perfect gift is from above, coming down from the Father of the heavenly lights, who does not change like shifting shadows." James 1:17(NIV)

God created us all for a purpose. To help us accomplish our purpose, He gifted us all with spiritual gifts and natural talents so that we can use them for His fame as discussed in the last chapter. Gifts are inborn God-given tools that help you to walk out your purpose. Talents are more physical and unique abilities. Discovering your spiritual gifts and talents is a crucial first step in this journey.

WE ALL HAVE GIFTS

The first thing you need to know is that we all have gifts. Yes, you too whether you feel gifted or not. The Bible says in 1 Peter 4:10 (NIV) "Each of you should use whatever gift you have received to serve others, as faithful stewards of God's grace in its various forms." This tells us two things. First, we have all received a gift. Second, the purpose of it is for us to serve with it.

It is in the process of serving and using your gifts that you get clarity on your purpose.

Next, our gifts are all different. Think about the different functions that body parts have. They all belong to one body, yet they each specialize in something. Our gifts aren't the same. Your gift may be like an arm that grabs and puts things together. Or, it may be like eyes that have the capacity of envisioning and seeing the depth of things. Regardless of what your gift is, it will never be quite the same as another person, even if they are similar in some ways. Our purpose of why we have those gifts makes the difference. Have you ever heard two skilled pianists play? As great as they both may be, their "sound" will be different because of their style. Embrace what you have!

Sometimes, multiple gifts and talents are given to us. This is wonderful and dreadful at the same time if you are not aware of why you are good at many things. Have you ever heard the expression "jack of all trades, master of none?" If you identify with it, I know how you feel! You feel you have so much in you and don't know where to start, so you do it all! Let me give you an example. Take a look at the below schedule.

6:00 am- Alarm went off.

7:00 am- Got up and dressed.

7:15 am- Flew out the door with to-do list in hand.

7:30 am- Grabbed breakfast.

8:00 am- Went to class.

9:20 am- Went to the library.

11:20 am-Went to career counseling session # 8.

12:30pm- Ate lunch.

1:30 pm- Finished tasks before executive board meeting.

2:00 pm- Met with a friend

3:00 pm- Checked out Martial Arts Club.

4:00 pm- Rested, wrote or worked out.

5:00 pm- Had dinner with friends.

6:00 pm- Napped

6:45 pm- Finished typing agenda for meeting.

7:30 pm- Led a meeting

9:30 pm- Attempted to do homework but socialized instead

2:30 am- Slept

This was my typical day in college. Every week I was in counseling because I would change my mind with what I wanted to do with my life, as if I really knew. Every week I would try a new club or wanted to do something different. Indecision was a reflection of my lack of "purpose" knowledge. I was impatient and scattered. It was an outcry of my inner confusion. Part of my frustration came from trying to categorize myself and box myself into

Indecision was a reflection of my lack of "purpose" knowledge.

one talent. I thought that would be the solution to my problem. Why couldn't I just be obsessed with Nursing? Or Teaching? Or Engineering? It was easy for me to see the talent of others, but not my own. I thought if I could not sing, dance, write, skate or understand computers that I had no gift. I mean only really talented people can do such things. Right? Wrong.

My problem was not a lack of gifts. I had multiple talents that would automatically go to work for me: speaking in public, organizing, counseling, planning, and so on. The problem was that they were dormant and I did not know what was really in me.

It was not until my senior year in college that I came to realize that my purpose was not found in a title or a specific career position, and that I was not meant to be categorized and stay in one place. I realized I was given multiple gifts to satisfy multiple purposes, but those gifts were unique for me. There are things I could do that nobody else could, just as there were things others could do that I could not do. I had to get myself out of the mindset of "I have no talents like other people do." Or "I am good at this and that but that is nothing valuable." The more I put my gifts to use, the closer I came to understand my purpose. We all have a different function, and we all need to function!

What are your gifts? What are your strengths? There are certain things that come easily to you, and even some things that always captivate your heart. Are there things that get you so angry that you feel the need to do something about it? What is it? What do others compliment you on? Is it your giving spirit? Your leadership? Your ability to breakdown and explain complex matters? Your creative hands? What? Once you can identify those then you need to nurture them, not neglect them.

NURTURE VS. NEGLECT

It's good to know that you have a gift right? That means there is something special about you that no one else has. But there is a responsibility that comes with having a gift. We need to be good stewards of what has been given to us. If we can't take care of it, how can we be trusted with more? With great power, comes great responsibility. That is the truth.

The best way to be responsible with your gifts is to first pay attention to what is in your gift bag. Then consider the different ways you can utilize your gifts. Acknowledge them and put them to use! For example, if you are really good at playing the guitar then you should be intentional about playing it every week. Play at a church. Start a band. Write songs. Record videos of your songs and post them online. Volunteer somewhere and play. Take a class to improve your skills. Maybe music is not your thing. Maybe you are good at outdoor adventures. Exercise everyday. Join a running or hiking group. Lead hikes. Sign up for runs. Win the competitions and keep improving the skill. Whatever the gift is, nurture it and share it with the world. Now

I understand some of you may be good at multiple things, but don't actively pursue ALL things. There is always one or two that nudge our hearts the most (at different times). Pay attention to that nudge.

Once you discover your most dominant gifts, you need to stir it up! When you stir something, it means you mix it all together until something is produced. Think of mixing ingredients when you cook. To make pancakes, for instance, you stir flour, baking powder, salt, sugar, eggs, milk, and oil. You can add more items according to preference. It is after you stir and cook that the pancakes are ready to eat. The same happens with our gifts. You have so many gifts inside of you. Begin to put them to use. As you stir your different gifts you will begin to understand the awesome purpose God is cooking in you, for His pleasure. Yummy! I smell success coming to you right now!

The mysterious dynamic about gifts is that even when you choose not to utilize them, other people will. Your gifts get on automatic and others will somehow nurture them! People you are surrounded by start to require your time! For example, if you have the gift of counseling/encouragement, naturally people will come to you for counsel and advice. Even when you are not in the mood to talk to people, and believe me I have been there, somehow you still counsel! Or even when you feel like you need someone to vent to, suddenly someone calls you to vent! Why? Their inner lack clings to your inner sufficiency. In other words, their emptiness expects your fullness to be poured on them. I remember being in college and struggling to find time to study. It just so happened that every time I set my mind to study for a three hour block, I would bump into someone in the library who needed counseling. Now, I am not a certified counselor but my gift of encouragement and helping others to understand their problems was constantly going to work without my consent. Empty yourself to be filled again.

Nurture what is already in you. It will grow. Have you ever seen the movie "Spider Man?" If you have not, please do. His purpose was to protect mankind by preventing destruction. The gift or "super power" he was entrusted with allowed him to do this. Spiderman did not need to find it out or search outside in the world for it. He had to get understanding so that he could execute what was in him. He had to nurture his gift! Imagine what would have happened if Spiderman had neglected to use his gift. Many would have died.

Their inner lack clings to your inner sufficiency.

Whenever you decide not to use a gift that is in your hand, especially when it's in need and being requested by others, you are neglecting your gift. As a matter of fact, not only are you neglecting the gift but you are depriving yourself from the satisfaction that comes from sharing what is in you. See, whenever you serve others with your gift, not only do they benefit, but you benefit as well. You feel spiritually full. Neglecting your gift is a big problem. Larger still is the fact that you become best friends with selfishness, greed and pride. I know it's hard to admit, but sometimes we are selfish, greedy, and prideful. I know I can be. Remember even though the gift is in your hand, it is not for you. If your gift is like the color red, the point is to fill a colorless life that is in need of red. Not coloring it, deprives both parties.

Now don't misunderstand me. Sometimes people with evil intentions will attempt to pimp your gift! That's right I said it. It seems like they need your "color," but it's more like they want it for their agenda. These are the people that want to gain something out of your gift. Think of businessmen, directors, producers, actors, and even friends who have done this. Their motive is clear: "how much profit can I get out of juicing this person?" They walk around thinking of ways to manipulate what you have for their glory, not Gods. Now this topic of pimping and manipulation is so deep that I can't go into it in this book. More of this is covered in my two following books: "Love: Give It" and "Truth: Speak it." However, you may be asking yourself, "how do you recognize a talent/gift pimp?" They will use three different tools (often times in this very order) to seduce you into their hands: flattery and exaggeration, over serving you, and dependency of them.

The first tactic that "gift pimps" use is flattery and exaggeration. Their words will blind you from reality because you make an idol out of your gift and begin to think very highly of yourself. For example they can say, "Girl, you are such a good singer. When you sing it melts the hearts of the people you sing to." "Boy, you have hands of gold! Every time you draw something I'm in awe. I would pay one million dollars for ANYTHING you put your hands on." Flattery will make you depend on your gift rather than God. Certainly, some people will encourage you and compliment you, but there is a fine line between compliment and flattery.

The second tactic they use is over serving you. Once they constantly tell you how great you are and how "awesome your gift is," they will do things that appear to be an act of humble service. For example, they may give you money to pay for some classes that will improve your skill, they may drive you to where you need to be driven, they may make phone calls for you to move you forward in your gift, or they may even sign you up for contests or public venues where you can showcase this skill. In the meantime, as this is all happening, they act as "volunteer coaches." *"Hey listen I signed you up for this contest. I spoke to all my people and I know you will be great. When you get there this is what you should do to win. And please don't thank me. It's the least I can do for such an awesome person like you."* BLAH BLAH BLAH.

Flattery will make you depend on your gift

What does all this do? It makes you depend on them. This is tactic number 3. You feel indebted to them. Soon they will ask you for favors and you feel the need to say yes because "they have done so much for you." In reality, they did it because they wanted credit for your gift as if they own you.

Don't get pimped! Guard your gift! Listen closely to the words people use around you. And remember, your gift cannot be lost or taken from you, but it can be dormant, hidden, and even manipulated. Have an eye out for that. And here is another challenge. Always check the intentions of YOUR HEART when you are in need of someone's gift.

GIFTS LEAD US TO OUR CALLING

Your gift in action will always keep you in the direction of knowing your purpose. As you exercise your gifts you understand your purpose, and as you walk out your purpose you arrive to your calling. A calling is an inner urge or a strong impulse towards a particular direction. You can feel called to a group of people, a cause, or a career.

Let's say my call is to be the greatest mountain climber ever and my purpose is to inspire others to reach greater heights in life, but I don't know that. All I have is my "gift bag." In it there is a pair of hiking boots, a rope, and some gloves. Maybe I don't know where to start, but I see I have a pair of boots. So I start to use my hiking boots. Before I know it, I begin to get perseverance and endurance. I start gaining confidence as I climb from hill to hill, and start to believe I can maybe one day go higher. I fall a few times, and it frustrates me, but I continue. Next I start to use the rope. As I use the rope I find that I now have the ability to grasp meaning every step of the way, so now using gloves makes sense. I need gloves to hold on. In doing this, I get the inspiration to climb higher and higher, because I can. I keep doing it without knowing that I am walking right into my calling. Get the picture? When I start to utilize what is in my bag, I begin to get understanding of what my purpose is, and when I start walking in my purpose, it will lead me to my calling.

> As you exercise your gifts you understand your purpose, and as you walk out your purpose you arrive to your calling.

Therefore it is important that I stay on top of the game in life without giving up. Why? Perhaps there are 10 more people out there also called to be mountain climbers and my actions will inspire them to climb higher, right when they want to give up! Just as this hypothetical example, we are called to do something. We have been equipped with tools to get there and our purpose is the why or reason it's even being done. In the last chapter we will take a deeper look at callings and platforms.

RE-CAP

In the first section you have knowledge of your purpose. You know something great is in you, but you don't know what to do with it. As you exercise your gifts and you build your relationship with your Creator, you get the revelation of the purpose inside of you. This knowledge pushes you to want to know more of your purpose and make sense of it. Know your Creator so you can know the gifts He has given you. Exercise your gifts and come to the knowledge of your purpose as you experience a continued intimacy.

PURPOSE REFLECTION

Look at the list below. What are the different "crayons" or gifts that have been put in your hand to color the world? Choose the top 5 words from each category below.

NATURAL TALENTS	SPIRITUAL GIFTS
Accounting	Administration
Adaptability	Apostle
Advertising	Celibacy
Art	Discernment
Athleticism	Encouragement
Bookkeeping	Evangelism
Brainstorming	Faith
Communication Skills	Giving
Computers / IT	Healing
Creativity	Helps
Critical Thinking and Decision Making	Hospitality
Drawing	Intercessory prayer
Financial Management	Knowledge and wisdom
Health / Fitness	Leadership
Human Resources	Mercy
Imagination/ Visualization	Missions
Initiative	Prophecy
Making Connections and Networking	Serving
Marketing	Shepherd/Pastor
Math	Teaching
	Voluntary Poverty
	Other:

Music
Negotiating Skills
Persuasive
Photography
Problem Solving
Project Management
Sales
Writing
Other:

LIVE IT TIP!

Send a text message or email to your friends and family. Ask them: What do you think are some of my talents and gifts? Add what they say to the list.

Part Two

Understand Purpose

UNDERSTAND PURPOSE

"...he who cherishes understanding prospers." Proverbs 19:8 NIV

In this part of the book we will focus on understanding purpose. Once we know purpose and its different components it is important for us to understand why we are the way we are. This section of the book involves 3 things.

CHAPTER 4: RELATIONSHIPS: WHO IS WHO IN MY LIFE?

"When Elizabeth heard Mary's greeting, the baby leaped in her womb, and Elizabeth was filled with the Holy Spirit. In a loud voice she exclaimed: "Blessed are you among women, and blessed is the child you will bear! But why am I so favored, that the mother of my Lord should come to me? As soon as the sound of your greeting reached my ears, the baby in my womb leaped for joy." Luke 1:41-44 (NIV)

In chapter 3, we spoke about having a relationship with your Creator. Relationships are crucial for the understanding and fulfillment of our purpose. Naturally speaking, a woman does not get pregnant alone, neither does she deliver alone. She needs a main "seed provider" and nurses to help her deliver the baby! Spiritually, the same is true. We are all pregnant with purpose, but we really can't birth it unless we are in a relationship with the One who created us first and then in relationship with key players that help us "deliver." This is why divine relationships are important.

A divine relationship is when God connects certain people together for a divine purpose. Naturally you probably would not be connected with this person, yet you are together because you feel something larger connecting you. There is a mutual understanding that there is something to be accomplished together.

When we read the opening quote, we learn that there is some type of special connection between Mary and Elizabeth. I'm sure we all know the story of Mary and Elizabeth from catholic school or cartoons during Easter! Mary went to visit her cousin Elizabeth. They had not seen each other for a while and both were now pregnant. Mary was pregnant with Jesus and Elizabeth was pregnant with John the Baptist, the man that would prepare the way for Jesus. Both babies were destined to have a divine relationship, like both mothers had a divine relationship. Elizabeth did not know Mary was pregnant, but as soon as Mary greeted Elizabeth, the baby inside of Elizabeth jumped with joy. Why? The greatness inside of Elizabeth acknowledged the greatness inside of Mary. Each baby had a purpose. They were not even born, but were already divinely connected.

A divine relationship is when God connects certain people together for a divine purpose.

The same happens spiritually. There are some people you meet who provoke an automatic click in your spirit. It's a feeling that cannot really be explained, but you are certain that the person is in your life for a reason. They activate what is in you. They inspire you. They make you want to live life! It is a mutual interaction. When you KNOW that there is life inside of you, it causes others to leap as well. Influence is inevitable when you are full of life!

Have you ever felt that? Are there people in your life to whom you are divinely connected that make you leap for joy? Divine relationships push you to move forward in your purpose. They encourage, motivate, and make sure your "pregnancy" is healthy. They rejoice with you and suffer the pains with you, even when they can't comprehend the magnitude of what you will birth.

Relationships play a big role in my life. I'm a natural born relationship starter and maintainer. My knowledge and understanding of purpose increases every year and most of it is because of my connections and relationships. You can be connected to many people (because of work, school, family, hobbies, etc...) but not necessarily have a relationship with them. Even though connecting with people is a natural thing to me, not all connections make me "leap" inside, or motivate me to seek a deeper relationship. Certainly they serve some type of purpose, but not all have that something extra. In the past, I wanted to have a special connection with everybody! Somehow, I was looking for a part of me in them. In retrospect, the people I were drawn to the most were those who taught me something about my purpose either by being transparent or encouraging me when I wanted to give up. Conversations helped me understand why my life was going in a certain direction.

Some divine relationships are only in your life for a short time and others for the long run. Recognizing the difference is important so that you can value that person during the time that they are in your life. Some connections reveal your purpose with the other individual immediately and others, only time reveals. I have met people, for example, and instantly knew what my purpose to that person was, whether it was a business or personal connection. Others are still part of my life and I don't fully know why. For instance, I met three wonderful Puerto Rican women in college who were key players in my spiritual development. That was the initial purpose. The way we met was nothing but divine. We all knew and felt we had something "big" to do together, but we didn't know what. Even when we wanted to give up on our friendship because we got on each others' nerves, God and His purpose for us, kept us together, truth be told!

Don't give up on those divine relationships when the road gets tough. It takes spending time in these relationships to come to an understanding of who they are in your life...

Don't give up on those divine relationships when the road gets tough. It takes spending time in these relationships to come to an understanding of who they are in your life and vice versa. Keep building.

Relationships are more important than we think. Your connections are crucial because they can potentially influence the way you develop and how close you get to your purpose. We have all had a significant other—whether it's with family, friends, a colleague or a significant other. However, not all relationships are healthy. Not every person is meant to be connected to you or have anything to do with your "pregnancy."Similar to the small amount of people in a delivery room when a woman is about to give birth. They could have been there when God first impregnated you. Maybe they were there during your first trimester or second, but they are not meant to enjoy what you birth. The reality is that a great deal of people can't handle the weight of what you are carrying inside of you. This is why you need to be mindful of who is part of your life while you are in the process of understanding more about what your "pregnant" with. In other words, do they encourage you in a way that makes you want to birth what God has put in you or does the opposite happen? You need to know this.

See a true relationship requires true intimacy, and not everyone is in a position to commit to you. Hence, they can't move your purpose forward. It's like having a box of crayons. You can have all the colors in the world, but only certain colors can color the sun. You can't just use any color to complete the picture. It would look out of place. The same is true for relationships. You can be connected to many people, but not every connection will highlight what is in you and provoke it to come out. Only divine relationships will. Let's add perspective to this concept by studying a positive and negative relationship.

RUTH AND NAOMI

The story of Ruth and Naomi can be found in the book of Ruth. It is such an excellent example of a divine connection. Chapter one gives us a synopsis of what the story is about. We learn that during that time there was a terrible famine going on and as a result Naomi, her husband and two sons decide to live in Moab, a common enemy to Israel and a pagan country. Naomi's husband dies and soon after, her two sons get married. One wife was Orpah and the other was Ruth. They lived in Moab for ten years and then both her sons died. This left Naomi alone with her daughter-in-laws.

At this point in the story Naomi decided to go back to her home in Judah because she heard the Lord was feeding them bread. She urged her daughters-in-law to go back to their mothers and remarry. Orpah left immediately, but Ruth stayed. Naomi continued to beg her but Ruth replied, "Don't urge me to leave you or to turn back from you. Where you go I will go, and where you stay I will stay. Your people will be my people and your God my God. Where you die I will die, and there I will be buried. May the LORD deal with me, be it ever so severely, if anything but death separates you and me. When Naomi realized that Ruth was determined to go with her, she stopped urging her." Ruth 1:16-18 (NIV)

Ruth had lost it all when she lost her husband. She had the option of going back to her gods and her people. Instead, the Bible tells us that she "clung to her." She chose to stay with Naomi! Ruth was determined to leave her homeland, her place of comfort, what she was familiar with and follow her purpose. She might have not understood what it was, but she was faithful to Naomi and remained near her. She knew she had to stay connected to Naomi.

Ruth was determined to go on a journey. There was something in her that was seeking truth, and she was willing to sacrifice everything to get there. Ruth's cleaving to Naomi is very moving. Her love for Naomi and Naomi's God kept her steadfast in her purpose. Later on in the story we learn that Ruth starts working in a field that happened to belong to Boaz, a relative of Naomi's husband's family. Check out the rest of the story!

> *"Then Boaz said to his servant who was in charge of the reapers, "Whose young woman is this?"*
> *So the servant who was in charge of the reapers answered and said, "It is the young Moabite woman who came back with Naomi from the country of Moab. And she said, 'Please let me glean and gather after the reapers among the sheaves.' So she came and has continued from morning until now, though she rested a little in the house." Then Boaz said to*

> *Ruth, "You will listen, my daughter, will you not? Do not go to glean in another field, nor go from here, but stay close by my young women. Let your eyes be on the field which they reap, and go after them. Have I not commanded the young men not to touch you? And when you are thirsty, go to the vessels and drink from what the young men have drawn"* Ruth 2:5-9 (NKJV).

Did you just read that! He took notice of her and soon they got married and had a son who is in the lineage of Jesus Christ himself. Purpose! What if Ruth would have chosen to go back to her mother? What would her future be like? She went from having no God to serving the one and only God of Israel. She married a mighty man of wealth and made Naomi very happy by giving her a grandson.

Sometimes we might not see the whole picture or have a clear understanding of what our purpose is, but faithfulness to the divine relationships God has placed in our life will get us closer. Who are those divinely connected to you? Are you faithful to those relationships? Know your divine connections and stay faithful to them; even if you don't understand what part of you they will help birth. And if things get tough, and they will, cling to them!

What does a Naomi look like?

- A mother who encourages you and pushes you towards purpose

- A person who gives you advice on how to get closer to your purpose either by listening to you speak and offering wisdom, giving you solutions to some of your immediate problems, or actually helping you reach your purpose (offering their gifts to you.)

Now, what happens if we stay connected to people who are not benefiting us? For example, what do we do if we are in a relationship with someone who brings us down and doesn't celebrate who we are meant to be? Let us look at the story of Samson and Delilah to understand the dynamic of a negative connection.

SAMSON AND DELILAH

The story of Samson starts in the book of Judges, where the Israelites were once again disobeying God. They did not consider all God had done for them; they were still worshipping other gods and were constantly given to evil deeds. God decided to punish them by putting the Philistines in charge of them for 40 years. The Philistines were a group of fierce warriors who lived along the Mediterranean coast near ancient Israel. They were very spiteful towards the children of Israel.

This is where Samson comes into the picture. Because his mother could not have children, an angel of the Lord appeared to her and said:

"For behold, you shall conceive and bear a son. And no razor shall come upon his head, for the child shall be a Nazirite to God from the womb; and he shall begin to deliver Israel out of the hand of the Philistines" Judges 13:5 (NKJV).

The first thing the angel told her was that she was going to conceive and bare a son. This was great news to a woman who was unable to conceive. It shows us that God is an expert at creating something out of nothing. He is the master of impossibilities, and there is always a purpose behind his actions. The angel then gave instructions to the woman. He told her that no razor should come near his head. In other words, he was not to cut his hair. The reason for this was because he would be a "Nazarite" unto God. The term Nazarite comes from the Hebrew word nazir which means "consecrated" or "separated. In ancient Israel those who wanted to be dedicated to God had the option of taking a Nazarite vow. The stipulations of the vow are found in Numbers 6:1-21 (NIV). *Google that and read it. It was a crazy and strict dedication!*

The last word the angel spoke dealt with purpose. He said "he will begin to deliver Israel out of the hand of the Philistines." Remember that I said in Chapter 1 that purpose is an action statement. Notice how the angel said he will begin, which indicated that the work will not fully be completed by him yet his purpose was clear. The birth of Samson was right on time! He was going to be a solution to Israel's current captivity. As Samson grew he discovered that he had incredible strength! He killed more than 1000 Philistines and even a Lion with his bare hands. Can you imagine? If I saw a Lion I don't know if I would play dead or run for my life, much less kill it with my hands! But God gave him supernatural strength to accomplish his purpose. It was his gift and he used it well! So well, that the Philistines hated Samson and tried to figure out the secret to his strength.

As the story progresses we learn that Samson decided to go to the Valley of Sorek, which means "Valley of Choices" or "Valley of Vines." Samson had choices. He didn't have to go into the Valley of Sorek, but he did and noticed a woman. "Some time later, he fell in love with a woman in the Valley of Sorek whose name was Delilah" Judges 16:4 (NIV).

> We know a person is slowing us down or taking us further away from our purpose yet we stay!

Delilah was her name and seducing was her game. That girl was poison! Delilah is a Hebrew word that means "temptress or seductive." Her name is also wordplay on the Hebrew word layla, which means "night." The night overcomes the sun, or Delilah overcame Samson, which means "of the sun." There is more to a name than what you think!

Since the Philistines already knew she was with him, they said to her, "See if you can lure him into showing you the secret of his great strength and how we can overpower him so we may tie him up and subdue him..." Judges 16:5 (NIV). Despite the fact that Delilah tried to betray him three times, Samson chose to stay with her. Aren't we like that sometimes? We know a person is slowing us down or taking us further away from our purpose yet we stay! This is detrimental! Run for your life before it runs over you! Sure enough, with persistence she seduced him and won him over. She begged him to tell him the secret of his strength and he gave in.

> *"And it came to pass, when she pestered him daily with her words and pressed him, so that his soul was vexed to death, that he told her all his heart, and said to her, "No razor has ever come upon my head, for I have been a Nazirite to God from my mother's womb. If I am shaven, then my strength will leave me, and I shall become weak, and be like any other man" Judges 16:16-17 (NKJV).*

Read the rest of the story. The Philistines came in and conquered. They took out Samson's eyes as mockery. Samson completed his purpose, but it cost him his sight and shortly his death. He did not live to see the fruits of his purpose fulfilled. God used Samson to defeat the Philistines, but had he obeyed, God could have used him for more. Samson had already been betrayed by his first wife who was a Philistine and he knew the Philistines were after him. Yet, he chose to pour his heart out to Delilah. He stayed connected to her and was lured in by her words. Some of you have been in connections that have destroyed you and defeated you. Like Samson, you may feel like you have no vision or gifts in life. But allow me to share a little secret with you. If you read the very last sentence in that paragraph it reveals something special. It says: "However, the hair of his head began to grow again after it had been shaven" Judges 16:22 (NKJV). What does that mean? There is hope! Those relationships may have stripped you from everything, but your gift will come out again! It cannot be taken from you. Be encouraged! Learn the lesson and keep it moving!

To whom are you pouring out your heart? What comes out of your mouth is a reflection of what is abundant in your heart. Be mindful of who you are connected to and who has your open heart in their hand. If it's not a divine connection, people will sometimes use your very words to destroy your purpose. Now I am not saying that everyone who is not divinely connected to you is your enemy. Neither am I saying that everyone is seeking to destroy your purpose. I am saying that not every relationship is Godly. Be mindful of your

> Be mindful of who you are connected to and who has your open heart in their hand. If it's not a divine connection, people will sometimes use your very words to destroy your purpose.

connections and who you give access to.

One of the ways to detect a negative connection in your life is to listen to the conversations you have. People whom God has placed in your life will always in some way or another push you towards your purpose. They will encourage you in your gifts, challenge you to grow, and speak life to you. If the person is trying to "cut off your strength," it is not godly.

What does that look like? Let's say God is calling you to be a singer and everyday you sing and write songs.

A Delilah in your life will manipulate you and put your attention in something that's not singing.

A Delilah in your life will consume all your time with meaningless conversations and pointless activities. A Delilah in your life will not encourage you to use, improve, or share your gift.

A Delilah in your life will control your friendship until they conquer their purpose: to distract you from your purpose and cut off your strength, weaken your gifts. Cut off those bad connections before you get cut!

What else is a Delilah?

- A best friend who is constantly envying you and distracting you from growing as a person
- A brother or sister who is always putting you down and shows indifference
- A boyfriend or girlfriend who constantly attempts to

"control your life" and suggest things you shouldn't be doing rather than things in life that are positive.

- A spouse who selfishly occupies your time with their agenda, rather than encouraging you to grow in your purpose together.

For those in a marriage, the solution is not to cut off your spouse if they show Delilah characteristics. PRAY for them because God can change things around and reveal what your purpose is together. Seek for purpose together. The gifts you have are to mutually benefit, satisfy and grow one another for the benefit of God. Take inventory of what you have. Think about your relationships for a moment. Who are the Delilah's in your life? Who are the Naomi's?

> Purpose begins in your relationship with Him. Then God puts you in relationship with people who will push you towards your reason of being.

Positive and negative relationships could cause progression or regression of your purpose, relatively. "Ruth and Naomi" relationships bring clarity and keep you on the right road toward your purpose. On the other hand, "Samson and Delilah" relationships can kill the very thing that wants to live in you; stealing your strength, vision and potential.

The main point is that God is a God of relationship. Purpose begins in your relationship with Him. Then God puts you in relationship with people who will push you towards your reason of being. Purpose is always connected to community. God never gives us a gift to keep for ourselves but He blesses us to be a blessing to others. Understanding relationships in your life, is one way of getting closer to your purpose.

PURPOSE REFLECTION

Fill in the below chart. Who are the Naomi's and Delilah's in your life?

NAOMIS (push you towards purpose)

DELILAH'S (pull you away from purpose)

1. Look at the Naomi's in your life: Are you taking care and committed to the divine relationships in your life? If not, how can you improve this? If yes, what are you doing that works?
2. Look at the Delilah's in your life: why are these people still in your life?
3. Are you willing to cut the Delilah's out of your life? If not, what stops you?
4. What is your definition of a friend, acquaintance, family, and brother/sister?
5. What kind of people do you attract into your life? Is it easy for you to maintain a relationship with them than any other person?

LIVE IT TIP!

Circle one of the Delilah's and Naomi's from your list. Do something today to build your Naomi. Make one decision today to cut off your Delilah (erase his/her number, throw out gifts given, etc...)

CHAPTER 5: THE PAIN OF PURPOSE: IDENTIFYING THE THIEVES IN YOUR LIFE

"No test or temptation that comes your way is beyond the course of what others have had to face. All you need to remember is that God will never let you down; he'll never let you be pushed past your limit; he'll always be there to help you come through it"
1 Corinthians 10:13 (MSG).

Life's struggles are inevitable. We all have bumps in the road. We all experience challenges. They're like that painful dentist visit we simply can't avoid when we get cavities.

Life happens. Things don't go your way. You miss some deadlines. People get on your nerves. You say you will not do something and you do it. You give someone your word, and you don't keep it. Your family starts acting crazy. Your money starts looking funny and all of a sudden, you are in the same rut you thought you would never be in. You cry. You complain. You vent and it hurts. You feel like giving up the moment life gets frustrating. Guess what, you are not alone. In fact, we have all been there! Life happens and it is uncomfortable.

If we don't tend to ourselves, it can be very dangerous

and if we let challenges get to us, we enter danger zones. The danger zone is a place where you are not in control of your mind and emotions, making you vulnerable and very susceptible to any kind of downfall. It is crucial to know whether or not you are in the danger zone because frustration can lead to desperation. While it's okay to talk about your desperation, talking alone will not make things better. Trust me. I am still learning to be proactive and move forward with my life after I get it out of my system. Ask God to help you in this area. If not, you open the door to different thieves in your life.

THE THIEF COMES TO STEAL, KILL, AND DESTROY

A thief is something or someone who robs you of your power and potential. Its primary objective is to kill your purpose. A thief does not come to play with you. A thief does not come to keep you company. A thief does not come to hear your problems. No! A thief comes to do damage!

I'm sure you have experienced this. You felt life was great. You had a steady job. You had awesome friends. You had an idea of where you were going in life and then it happened. You had a bad break-up, got in an argument with your best friend, found out a secret you wish you hadn't, had a family problem, or experienced something traumatic. These life experiences can make you feel depressed, fearful, and even doubtful. I have been there. Life events are designed to help us reflect where we are in our journey. We get humble. We think of the issues inside of us that otherwise we would be avoiding. This happens to all of us and it's not necessarily a bad thing as you will read later. But the minute you let those events take over your life, you have been robbed! Fear stole your faith. Depression stole your joy! Insecurity stole your confidence. Pride stole your humility and bitterness stole your gentle spirit.

While there are many thieves that rob us, for the purpose of this book, let's take a look at three of the most dangerous ones: fear, doubt and comparison.

IDENTIFYING THE THEIVES IN YOUR LIFE

Thief # 1: FEAR

You remember growing up; people would always say things like: "Keep the lights on, I'm afraid of the dark" or "I'm scared of being so high up, get me down!" or "Kill that roach it's getting closer!" There was always a fear of something; fear of the dark, fear of heights, fear of insects. The list can go on and on.

Compared to the spiritual world, these fears are nothing! Fears are internal mountains that can literally paralyze and destroy the success in our life if we let it! It can paralyze our purpose in God. Everyone struggles with fear in some capacity: fear of man, fear of success, fear of failure, fear of being rejected, fear of being abandoned, etc...

The first step in getting this answer is to ask yourself: in what area is my struggle? Then think back on what made you develop that fear. Oftentimes we see the outward problem, but we ignore the inward root. I won't go over it in depth in this book because that is a completely different topic. But I encourage you to figure out what fear, if any, is holding you captive. Understanding this inner part of you will make you victorious over this thief when it tries to convince you into aborting your purpose!

> Oftentimes we see the outward problem, but we ignore the inward root.

It took me a long time to figure out my fear. I went through a time in my life where I kept trying new things: opportunities, activities, projects, and more. Tasks got started, but never finished. The idea of finishing something was so terrifying that upon seeing the finish line, I would slow down, eventually stop, and quickly run away from it. I started to feel unsuccessful and unaccomplished which in turn made me feel somewhat depressed with my life. I would condemn myself because I did not understand my inconsistency. Have you ever been there? It's not the most comfortable place to be. So what did I do?

I got some counseling! Not the kind you are thinking. One day back in 2007, I heard for the first time somewhere that Jesus was our counselor. I never really approached Jesus as a counselor, but intrigued by the idea, I wanted to give it a try. That night when I got home I sat on the floor, took out my journal and Bible, and prayed. I was just rambling and telling Him what I was feeling and I asked certain questions. These are the questions I asked my Counselor:

- Why am I so inconsistent?
- Why do I start projects and not finish them?
- Why don't I give things my all?
- Why am I afraid to actually do what I said I would?

I waited in silence for a long time trying to sort my emotions and then like a rushing wind I began to write. As I wrote I was receiving so much revelation about me that I never knew about! Amongst everything written, I discovered that I struggled with a fear of success. That's right, I was afraid of being successful. I could not understand why, but God began to take me back, way back to my childhood and showed me the root of my fear.

Ms. Goody Two- Shoes

Growing up I was the weird girl. I was not pretty. My wardrobe was hideous. I wore clothes from a flea market and "hand me downs," because we couldn't afford anything new. School was my priority. I loved everything that came with the nerd package: learning, doing homework, my classmates, and asking questions. I was the kind of girl that would be friendly to everybody, but I would not get close to anybody. My closest friends were my cousins. We did everything together.

As I grew up, the family always viewed me as "the perfect one," and oftentimes would label me as "la santica" or "Ms. Goody Two-Shoes." I was a good student. I obeyed my mother. I was quite affectionate and loving with all my other family members. It made sense.

This was not good because slowly everyone was always compared to me. My cousins were compared to me. My sister was compared to me. Students were compared to me. Even when I entered my first relationship it "seemed" perfect. It was the first boyfriend I ever had, yet the way we "managed it" gave others the impression that we had years of experience in dealing with relationships! This was great in the beginning, but soon my family used my relationship as the standard for my other cousins. "Why can't your boyfriend be like Eliana's boyfriend?" Why can't you guys be like them etc...? My cousins slowly started drifting from me and we grew apart tremendously. These two dynamics of being called perfect all the time and the change in my relationship with my cousins did two things:

- I started to believe I was perfect
- I developed a fear/obsession to do things the right way all of the time.

MY ROOT THOUGHT WAS: IF I GIVE PEOPLE MY ALL, I WILL BE REJECTED.

Bingo! There was the root lie that started it all. That one root thought dominated ALL of my actions from that moment on. Slowly I started procrastinating in homework. I stopped finishing projects, and I stopped giving things my all, including people. I became more selfish in giving love because I subconsciously believed somehow I would be rejected if I gave it my all. I became more selfish with my time. I became more selfish in my resources. This went on for my entire college career! I would start off every class with excitement and on top of my game. I would get good grades and was even on the honor roll and Dean's list. But when it seemed too perfect, I would dumb myself down just to not feel successful. In relationships, if things were going "too right" I needed to find something wrong, because the idea of success even the smell of it— terrified me. See, but it was this very fear that was stopping me from fulfilling my purpose in all my different stages. It was this fear that was stifling my faith! Fear of Success!

> My root thought was: If I give people my all, I will be rejected.

The root of that was rejection and not feeling loved at a particular point in life. With time, it grew and what was visible was inconsistency, not following through, but it was deeper. See how one small lie opens the door to bigger issues? You may think the big tree you see is the problem, but it's always a small seed that starts it.

Root thought: If I give life or people my all, I will be rejected

The above diagram only shows one of the many root thoughts or lies I had. In the third book of this series, we will go more in depth about this, but for now, think about what is stopping you from your purpose? What fear is stifling your faith?

Maybe you fear failure. Perhaps all your life you made mistakes and you were made fun of. So now you are a workaholic, you go above and beyond because you think that WHAT you do is HOW you will be loved.

Maybe you fear man, what people think and say of you. You like to please people because it's your way of feeling validated and love.

Maybe you fear having money because the one time you did have it, you mishandled it. And as a result those around you distanced themselves and you felt abandoned.

Maybe you fear abandonment because growing up you were always left alone and not given attention, so now you feel the need to be around people constantly. You join a million organizations and get involved only to be around someone.

What is eating at you right now as you read this? Have you ever said this to yourself: "I will never amount to anything in life. Everyone has to like me. People will always let me down. I will never have enough money. I will always be poor. What if I stay alone in life? What if nobody wants me? What's my value?" Have you ever felt rejected? Unworthy? Alone? Abandoned? Misunderstood? Guess what. WE ALL HAVE!

I challenge you to deal with it right now. What is that fear? Kill it! Sit in a park somewhere. Get a pen and paper and think of your story. Change your thoughts right now. Instead tell yourself: "I don't have it all figured out, but God does. I won't be accepted by every one and that's okay. I am valuable and worth it. I am wanted and loved. I matter to God and others."

After you have identified those root thoughts, only the love of Christ can help you conquer that fear. Fear is the absence of love. Where fear is present, love is not. When we receive his love, fear cannot exist in us. "Perfect love drives out fear..." 1 John 4:18 (NIV). Not some of it. All of it, but love needs to be perfected in us. That is, the love of God, not drinks, money, honey's, or blunts.

> I don't have it all figured out, but God does...

THIEF # 2: COMPARISON

The second most deadly thief after fear is comparison. Can you admit that at one point in your life you have compared yourself to someone? After doing so, you probably felt horrible about yourself! When we are stifled by fear, we become inactive and as a result begin to feel unaccomplished. This feeling of not being where we want in life makes us compare ourselves to other people.

Comparison happens for two reasons:

1. We feel unloved and unworthy
2. We are not as thankful as we should be for what we have.

When you don't appreciate what you have, you start to look at what everyone else has. Or you wonder why you don't have it. When I was in college, I would say: "How come this person has it all figured out?" "Why did they get chosen?" "How is that person succeeding more than me?" The truth is, nothing is as it ever seems. This is an ugly place to be. You need to identify what gives you the tendency to compare yourself. There was a time in my life where I was not moving. Since I let comparison make a home in me, I did not realize that my immobility was the perfect ground for doubt to make a home too! So when I would go to sites like Facebook I suffered! The minute I looked at people's pictures and read about their success, I felt unworthy. I was mad at myself because I felt so much life was in me and I did not know what was "wrong with me." I did not know how to be myself. Comparison would strip me and made me so doubtful that I didn't want to do anything. Luckily, I temporarily deleted my account until I was

> I had to focus on living my life instead of dying through people's status updates!

focused again. I had to focus on living my life instead of dying through people's status updates!

Fear, doubt, and comparison are best friends. Fear will stifle you and make you INACTIVE. This opens the door for comparison and feelings of unworthiness. Comparison makes us doubt, which only makes us more immobile and unhappy! When we doubt, it means that we simply do not believe that something is going to happen in our lives. We don't believe God. We don't believe others. We don't believe that we are good enough to have an abundant and blessed life!

Don't get caught up in the trap of comparison. You and I could be called to the SAME vocation/career/occupation. We can even have similar gifts, but our story and purpose will be unique to use. That makes ALL the difference. You are special and have something unique to offer the world.

You are special and have something unique to offer the world.

NO PAIN, NO GAIN

The pain we feel in life will increase our dependency on God and make us humble. We are not as "big" as we think. While some life challenges cause inevitable pain, there are some events that are simply traumatic. So much is the hurt that we prefer death. I know what that feels like and highly encourage you not to avoid the pain. People have different coping strategies to avoid confronting pain: do more, spend more, accomplish more, travel more, work harder, etc.. It's self-deceptive. Get help and take time to heal. Here are some starter questions you may want to ask yourself.

- What lesson is God trying to teach me from this?
- What issues do I need to confront in me?
- What is still causing grief?

You can't aggressively pursue purpose if you are still holding on to pains from the past.

You can't aggressively pursue purpose if you are still holding on to pains from the past. Imagine past pain being as old, laceless, dirty sneakers with holes on them. How can you run a new race with old sneakers? It will always be a roadblock until you take them off, rest your feet and are ready to put on new ones. Think about it. Are you fooling the road, or yourself?

Some may blame God for their "bad luck" and never approach Him or depart from Him. It is not His fault. Remember, we may not be in control of the issues we encounter, but we are in control of the decisions we make. Ask yourself if something happened to you or *for* you. It's all about perspective. Keep in mind that your pain will bring worth to someone else.

PUSH!

You may not be where you want to be in life, but thank God you are certainly not where you used to be. Pain can keep us immobile, but everyday you must push towards your purpose. Fear will stifle your faith. Rejection will happen. But you need to push! Let the desire for change and greatness motivate you to fight until you make it. God wants us to come alive to purpose. Your responsibility is to push. God's responsibility is to bring out what He put in you. You might be asking yourself push what? How do I push?

Push past yourself!
Push past your thoughts!
Push past your laziness!
Push past what you don't understand!
Push past your insecurity!
Push past your sleepiness!
Push past people!
Push past negativity!
Push when it makes no sense!
Push when it looks like it won't work out!
Push with Faith!
Push through prayer!
Push with vision!
Push with excitement!

Push with urgency!

Push in obedience!

PUSH!

Relationships and the struggles you go through are all grounds for you to understand your purpose. If you are never tested how could you know what you are capable of handling? How could you ever know your value? Persevere in these times. Life will smack you in the face with all kinds of obstacles. But get up and fight. People will let you down. But get up and continue living. We can't expect perfection from imperfect beings.

> If you are never tested how could you know what you are capable of handling?

If the battle against you is great, it's only a clear indicator that what you will birth is that much greater.

Fight or Flight.

PURPOSE REFLECTION

1. Make a list of the different thieves that steal from you (e.g. comparison, fear, doubt, envy, over thinking, laziness, etc...). Talk to a close friend and discuss, how do these thieves get in?

2. What crisis have you experienced that made you feel like life had no meaning?

3. Identify all of the root thoughts in your life. These lies were either told to you by other people or yourself because of a bad experience. (e.g. Everyone is going to let me down, everyone is going to abandon me, I will always be poor, I will never amount to anything in life)

LIVE IT TIP!

Change your negative root thought and meditate on new positive thoughts that will change the way you live. Consider the below tree.

I can do ALL things through Christ who strengthens me!

My confidence is in God's Power

I have a purpose and I matter

Root thought: God loves me unconditionally despite my flaws.

CHAPTER 6: THE PROCESS TO PURPOSE

"Consider it a sheer gift, friends, when tests and challenges come at you from all sides. You know that under pressure, your faith-life is forced into the open and shows its true colors. So don't try to get out of anything prematurely. Let it do its work so you become mature and well-developed, not deficient in any way" James 1:2-4 (MSG)

In the last chapter we established that life challenges will happen and that we need to be aware of the different thieves that come to steal our purpose. In this chapter, we will look at WHY the process happens and what we gain out of our experiences. Both are important to understand.

Pain is part of the process. Process is part of life. Everything we do or want on Earth comes attached to a process. There is a process for picking a college, career, our first car, a significant other, and even traveling to another country. There is always a price to pay. Sometimes when you work hard towards a goal, you learn to value it later. Or when we spend the time cooking a delicious meal, you learn to savor every bite! Such is the case with our purpose. Each of us has a journey we "go through," and while some are painful and others don't make sense, they are key for purpose living. Why? Because process builds our character and character is a necessary ingredient for us to sustain our purpose. Process prepares us for purpose.

With that said, I want you to keep three key truths as you continue reading this chapter:

1. Process perfects/strengthens our character traits
2. Process makes us aware of our character flaws and pushes us to improve
3. Process makes us value our purpose when we are fully living it out

Character tells a person who you are and what you are about.

Let's talk about how character is built.

STRENGTHENING CHARACTER TRAITS & FLAWS

The American Dictionary of the English Language defines character as "the stable and distinctive qualities built into an individual's life which determine his or her response regardless of circumstances". This means we have inside of us both good and bad qualities that determine every decision we make. I like how Abraham Lincoln put it: "Reputation is the shadow. Character is the tree." Wow that's clear! People who get a bad reputation, probably have stinking character traits. Character tells a person who you are and what you are about. You can't hide your character. It will drip out of you through your actions.

Your job is to identify what your good character traits are and which could use some work. Then, be diligent and become better. Life will offer you opportunities for you to "grow" in those areas. Once you figure that out, then you can understand why certain events happen in your life.

Below is a chart with some of the most common character traits we should develop in life to have good character. I have provided a longer list with its definition at the end of the chapter. Don't get overwhelmed. I have also provided some biblical references for you to think more about these traits.

CHARACTER TRAITS

The below version used for all of the below scriptures is New International Version (NIV), unless indicated otherwise.

CHARACTER TRAIT	NATURAL TALENTS
Commitment	Revelation 3:14-16 (MSG)
Compassion	Ephesians 4:32
Discipline	Galatians 5:16-26
Enthusiasm	Ephesians 6:7-8/ 1 Chronicles 13:8
Forgiveness	Matthew 18:21-22/ Luke 17:3-4 Mark 11:25-26
Generosity/	Deuteronomy 15:7-11/Proverbs 21:13

Hospitality	
Honesty	Isaiah 33:14-16/ Psalm 15:1-2
Humility	Psalm 37:11/ Proverbs 29:23
Integrity	Psalm 25:21/ Zechariah 8:16-17
Love	Ephesians 5:2/ Romans 12:10
Loyalty	Proverbs 18:24/ Matthew 26:33-35/ Exodus 17:8-13/ 2 Chronicles 11:13-16
Obedience	Deuteronomy 12:28/Job 36:11/1 Samuel 15:22
Patience	Psalm 37:7-9/ Proverbs 15:18/ Isaiah 40:31
Perseverance	Romans 2:7, 5:3-4
Reliability	1 Corinthians 4:2-4
Respect	Proverbs 9:10/ Proverbs 13:13/Romans 12:16-18
Responsibility	Proverbs 24:11-12/ Matthew 25:14-30
Self-Sacrifice	Mark 10:42-45

Take a look at some of these traits. Circle the top 4-5 words that make your character good. In other words, which of the above traits have you been complimented on and you know you have under control? It may be your patience. Perhaps, others really appreciate how reliable you are. Or maybe you are a very loyal person. Don't take these great traits for granted. Take the time to learn more about them and keep deciding to be these things. Everyday you have to decide if you are going to be loyal, patient, or reliable (if those are your strengths). Let me give you an example.

One of my strongest character traits is hospitality. It's very easy for me to share my food, conversations and make someone feel welcomed in my home. It's a natural thing. However, I need to decide to be hospitable everyday. Suppose a friend made me mad in the morning. This same person was scheduled to come over to my house later that night for a movie with friends. If I choose to close my house off because I am angry, I am no longer allowing my hospitality trait to go to work. Instead, plans continue as planned, and whatever issues I have with my friend will be taken care of beforehand. Things will come in your way, but you always need to decide if your good traits will continue being good. Ever meet someone who was always punctual and because others were late they started to be late? See, it's very easy for your good traits to become bad. When good traits go bad in others, don't let the same happen to you. Decide better.

> When good traits go bad in others, don't let the same happen to you.

Circling our good traits is easy! We can brag about our good characteristics all day. But are you willing to be honest about the "not so good parts of you?" Everyone has flaws. We are not perfect. God uses those flaws to give us understanding about ourselves and to remind us that even when we arrive to our purpose, we can't do it without Him. Go back to the character traits list. Put a star next to the 2-3 areas you need to improve on, especially if you sense "life" is trying to teach you that lesson. Or what have those close to you pointed out? For example, if they have called you prideful, then it's an indicator that you need to improve on humility. If friends have told you, "you hold so many grudges," then it's an indicator that you need to become more forgiving. Analyze yourself and think about these flaws. What are the top 3 flaws you have? Write them out?

Anything bad in you can always be changed to good. Not perfect, but good.

________________, ________________, ________________

I have given you more space at the end of a chapter to further think about your flaws, but it's important that you are aware of your issues. These flaws could have developed as you grew up or because of what you experienced. So don't think they are with you forever. Anything bad in you can always be changed to good. Not perfect, but good. The key to improving what you are not good at is to be intentional about it.

Let's say you really have an issue with commitment. You don't commit to events and activities because your mind is always all over the place or you may be afraid of being held responsible for something. How do you improve this? Well first admit to yourself that you have this problem and think about where these tendencies are coming from. Why do you struggle with commitment? Is it because of something in the past? Or is it fear? Use the same questions I asked myself in the story I shared in the last chapter. Get to the root!

Next, decide to be committed. Start small. If you want to be healthy but can't commit to a gym, commit to doing some kind of physical movement at home for 20 minutes everyday, then increase. Maybe you will go to the gym 2 days every week, until you build that area in you. Of course, different life events will assist you in this. They may not be favorable events, but your character is surely being built as you live through them. Just remember that you are the one in control every time you decide how you are going to respond, not just react. The last thing I want you to know about flaws is that you will always have flaws. We as humans are incapable of reaching perfection. The key is in finding what your strengths and weaknesses are so that you can constantly work on them and learn to interact with people. You may get good in one area and still have work to do in another. This is our nature. Strive towards perfection, but don't expect yourself or others to be perfect.

Before we move on I want to share with you a story of my process in a specific area. Sometimes we have "seasonal purposes." This is when God has a specific assignment for you for a specific time for the purpose of getting you ready for the next aspect of your life.

After I graduated college in 2008, I did not have a job lined up. I went to Africa and upon my return, it dawned on me: "I am not going back to class in September. I need a job!" Well, the opportunity to work for a small business near my house was offered to me. I never desired an office job. In fact, it was the last thought in my mind. After much prayer and thought I took the offer. Initially I did not know what my purpose for working there was, other than the fact that I needed money. But, once I began working, I knew. It was obvious. My purpose was to help organize the business, add structure and establish a system to improve productivity. My gift of administration and organization would help me to fulfill that purpose. At the same time, I had different professional weaknesses that I needed to improve on. Working in this office helped me to develop that awareness about myself. Now why was this seasonal? Well, God did not have me there because he was preparing me to take over corporate America. Though there is a business woman in me, I know that is not my calling. But that seasonal purpose was part of my process. There were certain characteristics I was lacking that I had to learn. So while I was there to bless

Strive towards perfection, but don't expect yourself or others to be perfect.

someone else, God also used the time to mold and prepare me for the next stage in my life. The lessons learned were priceless and indeed vital to my maturity and character development.

Below is a list of some well known Bible characters. I have listed their traits as well as their flaws. They had amazing traits, but deadly flaws. Their flaws constantly got in the way of doing what God called them to do. Yet, they went through the process. In some way or another God prepared them.

CHARACTER FLAWS

PERSON	TRAIT	FLAW
King David	"A man after God's own heart" (devoted and strategic)	*Guilty of lying, adultery & murder*
Jacob	Intelligent	*Deceitfulness*
Esther	Courage	*Fear*
Peter	Jesus' right-hand man, bold	*Pride*
Jeremiah	Obedient	*Doubt*
Job	Trust in God, Faithfulness	*Poor choices in friends/arrogance*
Moses	Obedient	*Egyptian Pride*

Every successful and even biblical person went through a process. Don't make the grave mistake of thinking you're alone. Here is another tip—your "story" will not be like everyone else's. I can be a speaker, but my journey as a speaker and how I got there will be completely different from another speaker. Everyone is not destined to do what you are. If you study the journey of different leaders throughout history that impacted the world, you will notice how unique their journey was. People like Martin Luther King, Jr., Mother Teresa, and even Abraham Lincoln made a difference in the world. Yet, their path to purpose was special. Even the people I listed on the list had a process. Take Moses for instance. Here is a guy who was adopted by the daughter of Pharaoh at an early age despite the fact that his people were in slavery. He spent 40 years on the courts of Pharaoh leading and enjoying riches. But there came a time where he had to decide if he was going to live that lifestyle or deliver his people. When he chose to accept his call, his process began. Moses wandered the wilderness for 40 years. That's a long time! But God used that time to remove his Egyptian pride and all the book knowledge/ wisdom he had acquired. Why? Because when the time came to deliver his people, the world needed to know that it wasn't his country pride or knowledge who did it, but God in him.

Regardless of what your path looks like, your process is all about character. Process requires you to die to your self (your pride, knowledge, thoughts) so that something bigger can live through you. When you are in this process you gain understanding about God and yourself. I can't tell you the events that will make your process, but just know your process will be unique to you. Don't avoid it. Embrace it and pray you remain standing at the end of it.

NO SHORTCUTS

Oftentimes we want to rush to know our purpose and skip the process. If you don't go through your process and bear the weight that comes with it, how will you value your purpose? How will you understand the value of what you "birth?"

There are no short-cuts with God.

Have you ever taken the time to think how gold is made for instance? I mean many of us love to wear it and it's so valuable to own! But have you ever thought about the detailed process involved if you want to purify gold? Gold cannot be sold on the market unless it's purified. The procedure is very dangerous, so the refiner must be extra careful. There is a great deal of chemical mixing and fire that the gold goes through before it is ready. Every step must be executed precisely, or it can ruin the entire process! The journey to purpose is the same. Process purifies our character. Process builds our character. Process gives us understanding of our valuable purpose and life. Only God who is with us in the process can take the dirty part of us, mold it into something good, and show us off to the world.

There are no shortcuts with God. You either go through or you don't. When we go through and endure, our character is developed. But when we try to skip what God has put in place for us, there are flaws in our character that could be detrimental. These defects interfere with our ability to walk out our purpose.

> ...circumventing the process life has for you almost always results in a longer path you DON'T want to be on.

Your process is individual to you and there are no shortcuts. Many have taken shortcuts. They strived to get to the TOP at all cost, even moral misconduct. But guess what. Their character is not built. Which means the minute pressure comes, they won't be strong enough to sustain it. You can work hard to build a reputation and one character flaw can throw it all down the drain. I am sure you can think of public figures who experienced this. One day they are in the game with fame, the next day, they are down the drain because their character was leaking!

Whether we choose to go through it or not is our choice, but circumventing the process life has for you almost always results in a longer path you DON'T want to be on. Have you ever been driving with someone who told you, "Oh I know a shortcut?" Hours later you find out it was no shortcut at all! Cutting the path in front of you is cutting your character inside. It is so tempting to want to jump to the next opportunity, relationship, job, church, or career without our character being built. What lesson do you think you need to learn right where you are? What is being built in you? Our ability to make better decisions will influence our character. Just remember that it is in this stage, that you grasp an understanding of your identity.

Just remember that we all go through a process. Jesus did. He was in the wilderness for 40 days before He was launched into His public business. Jesus knew his purpose. He understood it and He fulfilled it. And guess what... He suffered too! The Bible says that He learned obedience through the things that He suffered. So we are not exempt. Ultimately the point of us being processed is for our character to be developed. And the point of character development is to completely die to ourselves. For if we live for ourselves, we can't really influence the world, but when we die to us and realize that something bigger is in control, true life begins.

A MIND TO WIN

As aware as you may be of your traits and flaws, the most important thing after that is to keep a winning attitude. Surely, it may be easy to feel discouraged when you don't see life is working out for you. And yes it can be frustrating to keep going through the same situations and not understand why. This is a crucial time where most give up on themselves and their purpose. But this is the time where you need to push yourself to think like a winner! What is on the other side of your process is always better than what you go through. As bad as the pain and heartache is while we are living through our process, the beauty and joy produced out of it can't be compared.

Prepare your mind to live purpose. You prepare yourself by being aware of what is going on in your life and taking the necessary steps to be ready. How have others walked in their purpose? What are the things you are lacking that God needs to develop in you? You choose to submit and be patient because you simply can't imagine how much worse or what else is really in you.

A mind ready to win says I'm ready
A mind ready to win says, it may get tough but I am going to push
A mind ready to win knows it is not alone
A mind ready to win expects opposition
A mind ready to win is prepared to confront the opposition
A mind ready to win knows falling is part of the process
A mind ready to wind knows that failing comes before winning
A mind ready to win, chooses to win before the process even begins.

RE-CAP

During the second section of this book, you should have developed a better understanding of purpose. Your relationship with your Creator starts it off, and as you get connected with people in a divine way, understanding increases. Relationships can be positive or negative. Though they have an effect on your purpose, relationships are not the only way to gain understanding on your purpose. You will experience life challenges that are part of your process. Developing your character during this process is necessary because it helps get rid of habits that might be a hindrance to you later. To every person there is a purpose. To every purpose there is a process. In every process there is pain. In every pain, character is developed and character is essential for sustaining that purpose.

Now that you are aware of what purpose is, and understand the different dynamics of living with purpose inside of you, it's time to learn how to birth that baby! How do you bring to life that which is in you and live it out for the rest of your life?

PURPOSE REFLECTION

1. What are your 5 strongest character traits?

2. What are some of your character flaws?

3. What is one way you can improve on these flaws?

4. What are some of the events in your life you have tried to take a shortcut on? What was the result?

LIVE IT TIP!

Identify one of your flaws and focus on improving it this week.

Part Three

Live Purpose

LIVE IT!

"Be patient towards all that is unsolved in your heart and try to love the questions themselves like locked rooms and like books that are written in a very foreign tongue. Do not now seek the answers, which cannot be given to you because you would not be able to live them. And the point is, to live everything. Live the questions now. Perhaps you will find them gradually, without noticing it, and live some distant day into the answer." - Rainer Maria Rilke

CHAPTER 7: WHY IS MY LIFE ON PAUSE?: THE MICROWAVE GENERATION

"But let patience have her perfect work..." James 1:4 (KJV)

Have you ever been bungee jumping? Or Sky diving? Ever sat on the front row of a rollercoaster? Or maybe something less radical like, dive in a pool? Think about it. Think about that split second before jumping into a deep pool. Think about the pause before a rollercoaster begins to go downhill. Think about the last breath taken before doing something crazy. Or the second before a basketball player shoots the ball to break a tie and win the game. Would you agree that before every moment of high adrenaline there is a pause? Purpose works that way as well.

The stillness always comes before the living. Or like I like to say it, there is always a "chilling before the livin." In an analogy of running, if knowing purpose is putting your sneakers on and understanding it is walking on the track field, then this part of the process is being down on ready position like a sprint runner before sprinting.

Another word for this might be waiting and when that is involved, it requires patience from our part. There is a quote in the Bible that says: "But let patience have her perfect work..." James 1:4 (KJV)

Notice how this scripture says let patience have "her" perfect work. It gives the word patience a feminine characteristic, which makes me think of a woman who is pregnant. When a woman is pregnant, the process of pregnancy has to have its perfect work before she delivers. The baby inside of her develops its different parts in different months so waiting for full development is important. The woman may want to give birth at 6 or 7 months, but despite the labor pains or her anxiety, waiting is crucial.

THE MICROWAVE GENERATION

It seems like before your "Big break", before hearing that gun shot to run on purpose, your life stops. This is the part that most people do not like because we don't like to wait. We want everything fast and now! We eat microwavable foods because we don't have the patience to wait for a good meal to be ready. We go to fast food restaurants because we don't want to grocery shop and cook. We buy bootlegged DVDs, because we don't want to wait for the movie to come out to watch it. We don't like to wait! We want things now! And we want it our way! When we go shopping and stand in a line, immediately we start looking up to the cashiers to see how slow or fast they are working. We run our eyes through other registers to see if there are shorter lines. We see people in front of us and start counting how many items they have. We either hope they have less than us so the line can go quicker or we hope they have more. Perhaps, they can take pity on you and ask you to cut them. Not in the United States! And hey, don't act like I am the only one who does this!

Indeed we are the microwave generation: "give it to me in 3 minutes please." This may work for hot pockets or popcorn, but not your life! Purpose is not microwavable! Discovering your purpose is like a marathon not a sprint. Discovering your purpose is ageless. Who said that by high school you need to know it all? There is no age or time frame to live out your purpose! We must have the right attitude when waiting for things to come together in our life otherwise its easy to get discouraged and give up! Things need to cook in our life. Purpose, character, our gifts, our story has to cook! If you can't wait you will be a raw product in the market trying to feed people what's in you. Who are you trying to make sick? Please wait. Don't settle.

We all have to wait before our "big moment" in life. Granted there are many defining moments we remember. I am more specifically talking about that memorable moment in your purpose path. Ask the man who took all the necessary steps to become a cop and needs to wait. Ask the high school senior who turned in all applications and needs to wait. Ask the woman who has built her life with a man and is waiting on the question or the man who has built his life with a woman and is waiting on an answer. Ask the businessman who has presented a very important proposal for an investment and needs to wait. Or finally, the actor waiting on his big opportunity. We all have to wait!

WHAT TO DO WHEN YOUR LIFE IS NOT MOVING

When your life is on pause it feels like you are not moving anywhere. It feels like nothing is happening. You feel like you have done everything to meet that last goal and nothing is working out for your good. This is frustrating. It could make you feel like your not really in control. Guess what? You're not. You need to remind yourself that your purpose is in the making. You will not understand or know it all at the moment. Do your part and wait for God to do His. When we have done all that is in our hands to do, faith has to kick in. Faith believes in the invisible until it becomes visible. Are you going to believe that the best will happen for you or will you allow the thief of doubt we discussed in chapter 5 to take over?

If you are asking yourself *"What do I do while I wait,"* there are two things I want you to know. While we wait for things to happen in our lives, we need to keep the faith alive and stay prayerful. Let's look at the life of a man who modeled this for us. His name was Elijah.

During the ninth century B.C., Elijah lived in the northern kingdom of Israel. At that time, King Ahab and his crazy wife Jezebel reigned. King Ahab was an awful king and his wife Jezebel was a manipulative seductress. Elijah was God's prophet and his purpose was to proclaim God's word so that Israel would repent and come back to God. He lived with power and was known for performing miracles. That was part of Elijah's abilities.

God told Elijah that there would be no rain in the land until Elijah commanded it as instructed by God. Elijah told King Ahab and he got furious! So what did God do? He hid Elijah in a mountain because he knew his life would be in danger. After three years, God told Elijah to go speak to King Ahab and challenge him again. It was time for the rain.

KEEP THE FAITH ALIVE

There is a verse in 1 Kings 18:41-44 (NIV) that tells us what happened after three years of no rain:

> *"And Elijah said to Ahab, "Go, eat and drink, for there is the sound of a heavy rain." So Ahab went off to eat and drink, but Elijah climbed to the top of Carmel, bent down to the ground and put his face between his knees. "Go and look toward the sea," he told his servant. And he went up and looked. "There is nothing," he said. Seven times Elijah said, "Go back."*
> *The seventh time the servant reported, "A cloud as small as a man's hand is rising from the sea."*
> *So Elijah said, "Go and tell Ahab, 'Hitch up your chariot and go down before the rain stops you.'*

In the above verses, Elijah went back to Ahab with another word from God. Elijah heard the sound of rain in the distance.

Remember Elijah had to wait three years before God followed through with His word. He was pregnant with God's word. Imagine waiting that long for something to happen? Elijah had faith that God was going to do what He said. Many times we don't have faith. It's hard to have faith and believe when it seems like nothing is working out for us. It even seems that God is indifferent. How can He say something and wait so long to give it to us? Well the Bible says God is not lazy or relaxed concerning His promises, so we need to keep the faith alive! Look at Elijah. Even when he only saw a small cloud, he believed that there was rain coming. His faith and obedience in prayer made God's job easier. God's job was to prove He was God and be faithful to what He spoke to Elijah in the beginning. Because Elijah obeyed and had faith, it sped up the process.

How can you keep the faith alive as you wait? Continue to speak what you are believing God for. "I believe God will bring me out of this situation. I believe God will bring me clarity on what I need to do next? I believe God has my back and will bring the right people into my life." Speak in faith and surround yourself with others who will agree with you and encourage you.

PRAY

Now if you are asking yourself what Elijah did as he waited, it's the second thing we must learn to do. He prayed! In chapter three we talked about intimacy. One of the ways to be in a place of intimacy with God is by talking to him. Have a conversation! In other words, pray. Prayer is a way to gain intimacy. Intimacy is a conversation with God. Like any effective conversation, it requires that you open your mouth and that you incline your ear to listen as well. In the text Elijah shows us that after God gave him the instruction to inform King Ahab on what was coming, and after he was obedient, he went to pray. He prayed to God. He went to speak to him. He did not give up until his prayers were answered.

Elijah continued to pray and his prayers touched the heart of God. Did you notice that he put his head in between his knees (like a birthing position) as he prayed? Sounds crazy, but his physical posture and spiritual attitude told God: "Birth it through me Lord. Birth Israel's revival through me." He heard the sound of rain and prayed it into existence by faith. His mind was on God. He was patient. He waited. That's the right attitude.

Why does that matter to you? Well, when God impregnates you with His purpose and you have survived all types of attacks, you still need to go through a waiting period. God always gives us instruction on what to do while we wait. We are to believe and we are to pray. Pray when it looks crazy. Pray even when you can't feel, see, or hear what you are pregnant with. Pray even if you think you don't know how. One of the things I do sometimes which began in my early days of prayer was to sit on a chair. That's right. When I want to have a one-on-one with God, I sit on a chair and put another chair in front of me. I close my eyes and I tell God to sit there. Then I talk like I would talk and vent to any friend. Except after I finish talking I shut up and listen. God always talks to me. His voice is hardly audible though it can be, but most times, you will hear a small still voice within you. It causes you to feel peace. That is God speaking. Prayer will touch God's heart and cause Him to move faster than He intended! You must pray and continue praying no matter what you see in front of you. Just be still.

STILLNESS VS. IMMOBILITY

Allow me to make one thing clear: waiting does not mean you become immobile. Being still is more of a mindset than a physical posture. So when I say be still, what I mean is let your mind and spirit be at peace waiting for the right timing for things to happen in your life. Timing is everything. In the next chapter we will go further into recognizing the timing for events in your life, but learn to chill and be still as you wait on God. Most people love to be immobile. They pray for a job and then sleep all day WAITING for God to bring one. This is not what we are to do. Pray for a job, yes. Then go and apply for some. Then wait. As you wait, follow up and send thank you cards. Then wait. See the difference. What should you do as you wait for your purpose to come together? Scope your territory. Take inventory of your gifts—what are your character traits, who are the key players in your life, and what do you envision for your life? Keep moving forward, as you chill inwardly. Remember, take a chill pill but don't become paralyzed!

Lets go back to the runner example I gave in the beginning of the chapter, When the runner is in ready position (like we are on this stage of waiting), their focus is on another level. They believe and trust that they will achieve the desired outcome. They think of their abilities. They focus their breathing. In their mind, they scope the territory they are going to run to mentally prepare for any roadblocks or hindrances they may encounter. For instance they may say, "Hmm, mile 4 has more hills than the first 3 miles, I need to moderate my breathing and pace myself accordingly to not get tired so quickly." We must do the same. Scope out the territory in your life and prepare to run. Let's look at how to identify that territory or platform in the next chapter.

PURPOSE REFLECTION

1. What kind of runner are you— a sprinter (rush through life) or cross country (pace and take your time)?

2. What are some of the things you are looking forward to in life that you know you need to wait for? (accomplishing one of your goals, getting married, starting your dream business, etc...)

3. What 2-3 things can you commit to doing as you wait for this to happen?

LIVE IT TIP!

Think of one thing or person that makes you very impatient. Practice patient this week towards it or that person.

CHAPTER 8: IDENTIFYING YOUR PLATFORMS

"For we are God's handiwork, created in Christ Jesus to do good works, which God prepared in advance for us to do" Ephesians 2:10 (NIV)

Have you ever seen someone in his or her "element?" I'm talking about the glow seen in the face of a gifted singer as he/she hits those high notes, or the smile on a dancer as they show their best moves, the serenity coming from an artist as they draw or paint, the animated face of a teacher as he/she explains a concept for the first time, or even the concentrated eye of a baseball pitcher as he prepares for the final pitch to win the game. A person caught in the essence of their purpose is a beautiful sight to witness. Better yet is being able to witness this in multiple places at multiple times. Wow. Imagine that sight right now. Broadway shows, live games, an orchestra producing such lovely sounds. Everyone is in his/her element. What if you were in your element 24/7? How will your life be different?

The hardest part to think about is completed: you have a better understanding of your purpose and know the gifts entrusted to you. Now what? After knowing and understanding your purpose, the next natural thing that will happen is living it out. Before doing that, it is important to identify the different outlets or platforms that allow you to be in your element. Platforms are outlets, roles, atmospheres, opportunities, or fields that serve as a vehicle for you to live purpose. Actually, they are temporary vehicles that drive you closer to your final destination (your final call). Holiday parties, school shows, a musical album or even a karaoke night are examples of platforms for a person who was born to impact people through singing. Blogging, writing for a newspaper, publishing books, or sharing personal written reflections are platforms for a person born to impact the world through writing. A college major is a platform for a student. A career is a platform for an adult. A title at any occupation is a platform. The role you play in someone's life is a platform. These outlets give the person the opportunity to do what they were born to do, purposely. If your purpose is like a crayon, then the different coloring books that require YOUR color are equivalent to platforms.

You may be asking yourself why it is important to "know your platforms?" Well, it is important because whatever platform you are on, your goal is to be influential. Remember what we discussed in chapter 2, our purpose as spiritual beings is to "chill with God," so that others are inspired to want to "chill with Him" too and be all they were born to be!

THE 7 PLATFORMS OF INFLUENCE

A few years ago I was made aware of a movement that's going on internationally called "Reclaiming the 7 mountains of Culture." The focus of this ministry is to do just that: reclaim the 7 mountains of influence for God. Prior to hearing about the movement I was already aware of the 7 mountains of influence through the organizations I was part of. For the purposes of this book we will refer to these mountains as platforms instead. In chapter 1 we spoke about purpose being an action statement. Purpose is something that is constantly in motion, whether we know it or not. Once you know your purpose and understand where you are in the process of life, the next important step is to identify what platforms you are meant to influence. Despite the facts that roles, titles, positions, a college degree, and careers are all platforms in some way or another, they can all be categorized into 1 of the 7 platforms mentioned below. These 7 platforms act as pillars in society.

In the next page are the 7 platforms of influence and their individual purpose. You can visit www.reclaim7mountains.com for more information.

PLATFORM	PURPOSE	CAREERS/ VOCATIONS
Arts & Entertainment	To influence sight and sound. Value and virtue will either be celebrated or distorted.	Actors, athletes, musicians, producers, artists, etc...
Business	To influence the marketplace. Where finances and resources are either used for God's work or selfish gain.	Finance, manufacturing, real estate/sales, health care, entrepreneurs, etc...
Education	To influence developing minds hungry to learn. Truth or lies about God's law are taught.	Teachers, administrators, curriculum writers, principals, etc...
Family	To influence family values. The curses or blessings will pass to future generations.	Family &Marriage counselors, social workers, psychologists, etc...
Government	To influence community and society. Evil is either restrained or endorsed.	Mayors, commissioners, school boards, political parties, lawyers, etc...
Media	To influence the perception of truth and falseness. Information is interpreted through the lens of good or evil.	Journalists, broadcasters, public speaking, marketing, radio, news outlets, etc...
Religion	To influence the foundation of faith. People either worship God or idols.	Apostles, Pastors, Evangelist, Biblical teachers, Prophets

These are the forces that shape society and nations. We all have a place in these platforms. We are called to influence a field. Why do we want titles in front of our names? Why do we go to college to get a career? Why do we want that job or work for that market? Here is why. There is an inborn desire in us that wants to be influential and make a difference in life. Think about the wealthiest and most powerful people in the world right now. They all occupy the top of one of the 7 platforms. My intention is not to address whether they belong there or not or the spiritual meaning behind it. I want you to think about which field you are called to influence. If you acquire that, you too can live with POWER.

I know it's hard to think above your career or major. But you must think bigger! Endless are your possibilities! Society doesn't train us for big picture thinking. From the time we enter school, the entire world wants to know what we want to do in life. It's almost like a desperate desire to put people in a box! It starts out as sweet curiosity in elementary school with the famous question: What do you want to be when you grow up? It continues as an annoying reminder in high school with the famous question: "What college are you going to and what will you major in?" Then, when you are about to graduate college the question becomes, "Where will you work? What is your plan after graduation?" Don't you just want to yell, "LEAVE ME ALONE! IM TRYING TO LIVE AND FIGURE MYSELF OUT!" I would if I was you. Life is a process. Don't feel forced to give an answer or to say, "I don't know."

How awesome would it be if our questions would change

to, "What do you think your call and purpose is? What are your gifts?" If students can be encouraged to put their gifts to use at an earlier age, they would have a better sense of who they are by the time high school comes. There would be no need for a separate group called: G and T or "The Gifted and Talented," because everyone will qualify for it. This of course will require an entire paradigm shift in the American educational system! For now, be part of the solution by identifying where you belong based on what God has told you or taught you in life.

Think about your gifts and your "purpose statement," you must identify where to utilize them. For example, my purpose is to communicate God's love, truth and purpose so that others can come to an understanding of who they are and where they belong. I know I am called to the platform of Media, Education, and Religion. Within those platforms I function in the role of a Substitute teacher, an entrepreneur, a speaker, a writer, a servant leader, a counselor, and much more. These roles help me to satisfy my purpose. Think about yours.

You may be called to one, two or 3 of these. But as you grow with God the clarity of which specific platform you were born to influence becomes evident. Think about your life. Think about the job you have now or the major you are pursuing or want to pursue. Think about your current situation and life experiences. Where do you see the majority of your "temporary platforms" falling under? List your Top 3.

1. ____________________
2. ____________________
3. ____________________

If you have already identified your platforms, I want to challenge you!

If you are in the platform of education, are you influencing it? If you are a teacher, are you teaching the students with wisdom? If you are an administrator, is your hearts motive to prepare these students to go out and influence the world, or are you more caught up with your image and "position"? Are you teaching truth?

If you are in the platform of arts and entertainment, are you bringing out the value in what you do? Or are you distorting and perverting what you put your hand on? Are you producing songs that motivate and inspire? Or lead others to suicide? Are you producing movies that will change nations or are you leading people to immorality?

If you are in the platform of business are you too caught up in the prosperity movement or teaching others how to build wealth? Are you striving on your self by taking advantage of the lack of strategy of others, or are you teaching others how to fish?

If you are in the platform of family, are you being a role model in your family? Are you practicing healthy habits that will bring blessings to generations to come? Or are you cursing future generations because of your reckless living?

If you are in the platform of government, are you making wise decisions that are going to positively influence society and communities? Or are you sliding in your agenda even of people get hurt in the process? Are you setting the standard with policies and servant leadership? Or are you tainting the standard and selfishly leading?

If you are in the platform of media, are you distributing information righteously? Or are you manipulating the information to teach lies? Are you exaggerating the truth? Or speaking it for the sake of growth in others? Are you writing God inspired pieces of art that are mobilizing people? Or do they slowly keep people living in their fears?

If you are in the platform of religion, are you teaching people how to worship and love God in Spirit and in Truth? Are you bringing others into God's kingdom? Are you loving and living by His truth? Or are you perverting your title and position? Are you making yourself a leader where God hasn't told you to lead? Or are you manipulating God's people for your selfish ambitious gain?

This topic of platforms and influence is much deeper. I encourage you to read up on it. For now, just know you were born to operate in one or a few of these. Make it your mission to be more aware of the role you play and where you are called.

Recognizing what "platform" you will be most effective

in is crucial, because if you are not in place it can literally change the entire dynamic of society. Have you ever seen a person who is naturally funny and born to entertain people, attempt to be a business man or teacher? Or a person with no comedic talent attempt to be a comedian. They are out of place! Not being in place is dangerous. It will affect someone at a global level. Stay in place. Think about this. Let me give you a very dramatic example.

Think back on your high school cafeteria. You have a big room full of white tables. There are three vending machines on the top right hand corner by the lockers. Some students from the last period are rushing to close their lockers.

On one side, there is the famous pizza station and French fries area. Right next to that, we have the sandwich area and salad bar. And right in front of that, we have the hot foods area. Its Monday so today's special is Spaghetti and Meatballs! A lunch lady is standing by each register waiting to check tickets or collect money. The bell rings, students rush in, drop their stuff on their tables and rush for food. They are hungry! Let's imagine that Maria, one of the lunch ladies—her purpose in life is to serve food in such a cheerful way that others are inspired to serve. Remember purpose is an action statement. She has been given the unique gifts of hospitality, giving, joy, and even administration. Everyone is ready to eat, but there is one problem. Instead of being on post to serve food, Maria decides to carry a nasty attitude as she picks up garbage from the floor and places it in the trash. She thinks cleaning is her purpose and so she is not in place to do what she really needs to be doing: serving!

Because she was not in place, students could not get served the food they needed to eat. As a result, there was confusion in the atmosphere and other people got out of place, because they felt the need to fill in the missing gap. Time was lost. The other lunch lady could not charge people for the hot food that was supposed to be served on that day. Because no money was made that day and the school did not meet their daily quota, the usual amount of money they take out monthly to donate to starving children in the Middle East was not sent. As a result a mother in the Middle East prostituted herself in order to get money to feed her child who was reaching starvation. Another mother committed suicide. Another mother put her child up for adoption while another family stole food. All being scarred one way or the other even until their death.

This is a dramatic scenario, I know. But, it occurs everyday in schools, the business world, and even church. There are some people you work with or maybe you go to school with and YOU know that they are out of place. In other words, they can prosper faster somewhere else. Don't fall under that category. You have no idea how your out of order actions are negatively influencing someone else around the world. Walking in your purpose should produce an automatic joy. When you are in the wrong "platform" or not living on purpose, you live a frustrated life. You are not happy. You get depressed. You question your existence. You may even feel helpless asking yourself, "Am I the only one going through this right now?" You are not! And I don't want you to stay in that category either. Your frustration is the direct result of being out of place (physically, emotionally, or spiritually) Choose better. Also, when you are walking in your purpose you don't need to compare yourself with others because you are content doing what you are doing. Think of a coffee maker. A coffee maker is very content making coffee because that is what it was created to do. It does not get mad when it sees that it cannot heat up food like a microwave.

> Walking in your purpose should produce an automatic joy.

Decide today to identify your platforms and pray that God will show you the roles you are to play within them. Being responsible over your roles will help you as you do this.

DAILY ROLES AS PLATFORMS

Before we move on, I want to highlight the importance of roles. This is oftentimes an overlooked concept, but the daily roles you have also serve as vital elements for your purpose. Roles prepare you for your purpose. Some of you may be mothers, dads, daughters, sons, sisters, brothers, entrepreneurs, professionals, or students. We may look at these roles and the responsibilities that come with them as a heavy burden, but it's preparation. Trust me! For example, any athlete will tell you that their role as an athlete gave them discipline and focus, which as a result prepared them for anything else in life that required those two important assets. I used to look at my role as a sister as burdensome because oftentimes it felt like I had to be more of a mother than a sister. But when I decided to be a sister to my sister, I learned that this was preparing me for my purpose and the many other young women I would become a sister to. Think about the different roles you function in right now. Rather than overlooking them, think about what characteristic and lesson you can learn by doing them well. Don't take off your roles before time, and don't put on roles you don't need to. For example, some of you ladies may have a boyfriend and are playing the role of a wife to him. Is there a ring on your finger? Is there a written contract binding you together? Has there been a wedding? NO! So why burden yourself with extra responsibilities that are not yours to bear? Know what is what in your life. Otherwise it's confusion to the mind and suicide to your soul. Same applies to you gentlemen. Why are you financially providing and taking care of a woman who is not your wife?

> Don't take off your roles before time, and don't put on roles you don't need to.

I wrote out my "roles statement" and I look at it every so often to remind myself what I am and what I am not. Here is my role statement. At the end of the chapter there is space for you to write your statement. Read it to yourself daily. It is important to remind your brain who you are, who you are not, and what you are becoming.

> *"I am a maturing Christian woman currently in the process of redefining what serving and loving Christ is really about. A daughter who is learning to love her mother unconditionally. A sister learning patience and tolerance through her blood sister. A lover of God and his creations. A warrior in disguise. A student of life and spiritual truths. A life teacher and counselor to students and those she encounters. An accountability partner and best friend to a few women. An extrovert who has to balance between how much to give to relationships and alone time to receive from God. A shy neighbor who needs to interact more with the floor. An entrepreneur who is learning the discipline of stewardship. A missionary always ready to go on a purposeful expedition. A deep poetic soul seeking ways to express ideas, thoughts, and observations. An author and speaker in the making. I am not a wife or a mother, but one day I will be."*

As you write and read these roles to yourself just remember this, you are not your roles or your title. Your purpose is more than that. Look at Jesus. He had many roles and titles, but His name is Jesus and his purpose was clear. Roles are a platform for you to practice purpose. Your career or occupation WILL not define who you are. Perhaps your purpose is to teach others how to think strategically. If that is your sole purpose in life, it does not matter if you were in a school, a business office, or a college, your desire to teach others how to think strategically will be evident in everything you do. You will be that person who listens attentively and then offers another solution that forces people to think carefully about what they are doing. Hence a person can't say, "my purpose is to be a math teacher" just because they function under that role. They may be functioning in the role of a math teacher but that is only a venue for what they are meant to do. Teaching is their gift, not their purpose. If purpose were equivalent to sneakers or sports shoes and roles were equivalent to a field (whether it's baseball, track, football or soccer) then this means you can run and use them anywhere! I have spoken to individuals who say at the "field", "this is my purpose." But when we look to a field to define our purpose, we limit our mindset. Take the limits off!

Some of us get so wrapped up into titles and roles. I have encountered so many people that walk around saying," Well I am the supervisor of this company," or " I am the District Regional Manager of this and it is in my hands to make ALL decisions." Be very careful with getting caught up in your role and title. A lot of times people who do this are really afraid to be themselves so they hide behind their title. *Yes I said it, fear once again.* When I was a Minister at my former church I allowed that title to consume me so much, even though I hate titles. But because everyone would address me as such, it became more of a reality. When all that was taken away, I realized the title was just a comfort thing. What will it matter when you die what titles are in front of your name or what your GPA was? I am not saying that one shouldn't strive for education and be smart. But when we put our sole focus on these things, believing that our purpose and being is because of those things, we rob ourselves of the opportunity to experience life. Your purpose is not JUST to be a student, wife, husband, friend, but more. What is that more for you?

As you think about roles and platforms just know this: purpose is something you carry in you, not a place you go to (e.g. my purpose is to teach, not to be a teacher. Purpose is what I do and why I do it not what role I am in).

HOW DO YOU KNOW WHEN TO MOVE ON?

This section of the book was probably the hardest to write. I intentionally left it for this chapter because it is very important that we understand when to move on. This is often hard to do if there is an emotional attachment involved. So, in our addiction to the attachment we ignore what we know. There is no way we can live on purpose continually if we are still stuck on a career, relationship, title, role or idea. In my conversations of purpose I often get the question: "How do I know when to move?" Have you ever asked yourself that question? You may have when you think about relationships or your jobs. Those two areas are the most common areas that people want an answer to that question. In chapter 4 we spoke about relationships and identifying who is who in your life. I said that it is necessary to know why a person is in your life. What purpose or reason do they serve? Just like some relationships have a time limit and reason in our lives, "platforms" are the same. You need to know the season and the reason of why people and certain platforms are in your life. What is the right time? What is the purpose of what you're in? Remember platforms are like temporary vehicles. Reason and season is the same as time and purpose. Knowing both is critical. When I say season I don't just mean: Fall, Winter, Spring or summer. Season is the temporary time frame that something is supposed to happen or be completed in your life. My season as a college student was the 4 years I was there. Seasons come and go. They are not permanent. Let me give you an example.

Jesus was born to die on the cross so that He could save the world. That was His purpose. He fulfilled it when He died the cross as a blameless sacrifice that was acceptable in the eyes of God. Even though He knew His purpose, it took a process of 3 ½ years for his season to come. The time prior to His purpose being fulfilled, He was training the disciples, performing miracles to prove that he is the son of God, preparing for his season. So even though Jesus was clear with His life's purpose from the beginning, He had to go through a process before His "time" came. His greatest platform was THE CROSS. However, the different platforms during his process were necessary before the final stop.

He held the role of a teacher, prophet and missionary. He had the title of The Messiah, the Christ, miracle worker and Carpenter. He played these roles in synagogues, different cities, temples, houses, etc… All were platforms.

Imagine if one day Jesus would have said: "You know what…being a carpenter is pretty fun. I feel comfortable building stuff all day. I get to work out my biceps, be close to home and show off my work! I want to do this forever!" What if He chose not to move on when He had to? Christianity would be very different today. Thank God He knew and understood His purpose and He knew when it was time to move on. Think about the titles, roles, majors, positions, or relationships you are still holding onto. Don't make permanent what was made to be temporary in your life!

If you are asking yourself, "Well, how do I know when to move on so that I continue to grow in my purpose?" Here is the best answer I can give you from my experience: if you are in a job that makes you feel dry, unmotivated, and dead those are clear signs that the time is at hand. However you need to ask yourself this: Why am I working here? What do I need to accomplish here? Is this part of my process? Is God trying to develop some type of characteristics in me? Is there a connection I need to make with someone here? Is there a skill I need to learn that I will need for later on? If some of those questions are still in progress, it is not time for you to move, as bored or hopeless as you may feel there. Of course there are some uncontrollable situations that force you out of place, but even that will work for your good. I advise you to wake up and look at your situation through the eyes of purpose! Encourage and motivate yourself daily. Look in the mirror in the morning and say:

> *"Today is a great day! I will be productive at work (or school). This is only temporary. I will not be here forever. This is only preparing me for my life on purpose. People will get on my nerves, but I will be patient. Everything may not go my way, but I will do my best to do my best. I will talk to whoever I have to talk to. I will keep my eyes opened and ears attentive to learning the skills that are going to set me apart. I will stay focused on the bigger picture, while living in the moment. Today is a great day!"*

When I graduated college, I felt satisfied because I had the opportunity to do everything I wanted to do. Had I stayed another semester just because, I would have been miserable, because nothing in my mind, body, or spirit desired to be on a college campus. I knew it was time to move on. When you feel peace and satisfaction, then you know it's time to move on. On the other hand when you feel what I mentioned before: frustration, dryness, and you know you are NOT GROWING, RUN FAST. Never leave a place out of frustration or desperation. Push through it. At the same time, when it is time to go, MOVE IT! Don't let that fear we talked about in Chapter 5 keep you immobile. Staying in a place where your time has expired is like drinking rotten milk! It stinks, it's sickening, and it will rot your insides!

In the beginning of 2011 I had to make one of the hardest decisions I have ever made in my life: leave the church I was attending. This is the church that taught me most of the things I learned about God. This was the church that allowed me to experience the intimacy of God and the joy of growing with a spiritual family. This was the church I was attached to thinking my purpose was in it. But this was also the church that spiritually raped me and allowed me to experience pain and hurt. It was time for me to leave. You see I was utilizing my gifts and serving in many capacities for four solid years. It came to the point where I was doing things out of obligation and not love. Though I had many platforms in the church that brought better understanding of my purpose, I was greatly deceived. I thought I was a woman of purpose, but really I was a woman of fear and religion hiding under the skirt of the church. When its skirt fell off, I was left naked, but in a position where I was now forced to face my nakedness and reality. When I left, I cried. I felt broken. I was torn and hurt! I thought to myself, " God I have no purpose. What am I going to do now? Where do I go? Everything was a waste!" And God with a loving and gentle voice said: "I want you to live out your purpose Eliana." From that moment forth, with faith as my new best friend I experienced the power of daily purpose living! The pain became joy. The frustration became motivation. The bitterness turned into forgiveness, and the desire to LIVE WITH PURPOSE, ON PURPOSE was birthed.

PURPOSE REFLECTION

1. Below I have given you space for you to list the gifts you identified in Chapter 3. Think about the roles that you have and the possible Platforms they fall under.

GIFT/TALENT ROLE PLATFORM

GIFT/TALENT	ROLE	PLATFORM
e.g. Teaching	e.g. Teacher	e.g. Education

2. Write out your role statement.

____

____

____

____

____

____

____

3. Do you currently feel out of place in the job you're in? The major you have chosen? The title you have been given? What makes you feel out of place?

4. What platform or environment do you think will fully utilize your gifts and talents based on your past experiences? Where is it easy for you to be "in your element?"

LIVE IT TIP!

Look at the chart with your gifts, roles and platforms. Think about the Big Picture in your life and where God may be leading you. Draw what you see or write how you see this all coming together.

CHAPTER 9: BE AN ACTIVE INGREDIENT

"Whatever your life work is, do it well. Do it so well that no one else could do it better." Dr. Martin Luther King Jr.

Congratulations on making it this far! Take a nice deep breath and stretch. It's about to get hot! So you know and understand purpose better, but... Now what? What happens when you bring to life what God placed in you, whether it's a song, an album, a book, a business, a ministry, or your life? Well, you will experience that answer when you get up and become active!

In the last chapter we spoke about identifying your platforms. Once you know the "fields" you can run in, then the next step is to run! Be active! Get busy!

GET BUSY!

We all crave to live a meaningful life. We fill ourselves with knowledge and the latest "how to's" and sometimes get nowhere. Why? Knowledge alone is not enough in life. There is a famous quote that says "knowledge" is power, but I say the application of that knowledge is where the power lies. If you think not knowing your purpose is frustrating, think again. Knowing your purpose and not putting it to use is deadly! You have come this far, don't abort what's in you. Get up and live it!

We quench the thirst for meaning and purpose when we move from knowledge to action. When you know your purpose you feel empowered to change the world, but when you put your purpose to work, everything in you is satisfied and you change the world through your daily encounters. When you begin to live on purpose and for purpose, it provokes the purpose in others to come out. If you are a gifted singer for instance, and you have the gift to sing but have yet to discover it, every time you sing and give it your all, it will move something inside of me. It will make me want to sing! People who live purpose inspire others to seek purpose. Seek it. Live it. Inspire it. When you are an active ingredient you live relentlessly. There is no time to be stagnant because you are constantly on the go. Jobs come and go, but no platform is meant to be so permanent. Like a crayon, you must be ready to color at all times, even if the pages change, even if you are given a new book. Be an Active Ingredient.

Of course change has to happen in us first before we can go out there and change the world. But when you hold your crayon of purpose with faith and confidence, you can color with no fear! Be active and know without a shadow of doubt that purpose is in you!

If you are currently in your house please walk over to the bathroom right now. Don't worry you are not doing anything crazy! If you are not home you can do this later or see if you can find any of the items I am going to list. Do you see any mouthwash? Deodorant? Hairspray? Or anything with one of those labels on the back?

Pick one of those items. If you look on the back of the bottle where the "drug facts" are you will see that it tells you what the active ingredient is for the product and its purpose. For example, I have in front of me a bottle of mouthwash I got from Wal-Mart. The first word under Drug Facts is Active Ingredient. In this case, the active ingredient is Sodium Fluoride. Right next to it is the word "Purpose." The purpose of sodium fluoride in this mouthwash is: anticavity, or "to prevent cavities." Never noticed that before right?

You are like that bottle. Think about it. If you are the active ingredient to a bottle, what would be your purpose? To disinfect, to prevent, and to cleanse for product use. But for you, maybe it's to change, to influence, to bring, to make, to impact, to teach, etc... You need to know that despite the condition of the "bottle" or whether or not the "product" is used, the ingredient in you is active, waiting to be used! At the end of this chapter I have given you a handout to fill in your blanks. I have also given you what mine looks like! What is my point? You are a change agent. Therefore, be an active ingredient! If you KNOW you, then

DO you.

Get BUSY! Now I am sure that it can be challenging to find ways to busy yourself. But when I say get busy, I don't mean waste your time with meaningless agenda items. The point of "getting busy" is to constantly be in action towards your purpose. Utilize your gifts. Volunteer somewhere. Think about the things that move and provoke in you a feeling of desperation to get up and do something. What breaks your heart about the community in which you live? The homeless? The addicts? The abused? The mentally ill? The fatherless? The orphans? Injustices? What?

The world is waiting for you to live on purpose. Give of yourself. Serve. Love. Live. Everyday is an opportunity to live with and on purpose.

The world is waiting for you to live on purpose. Give of yourself. Serve. Love. Live. Everyday is an opportunity to live with and on purpose.

When you are walking out your purpose your whole life changes. For one, you help others get to theirs. Because you have the knowledge of your mission in life, it helps you see other peoples mission. Your day-to-day interactions change. When you are in place, it moves others to be in place or find their place in life. We desire to know our place and be in place. We do. Nobody walks around purposely desiring to be lost or out of order. If you do, please get some help! Our greatest productivity comes when we are in place. Our greatest accomplishment comes when we are in place. Our greatest sense of fulfillment comes, when we are in place. Get in place with God. Impact happens when you connect yourself to people who know their purpose and know their place in this world. We are a community, an organism. Each of us serves a function and we benefit from each other's function. The eye needs the head as much as the fingers need the hand. Independently we get NO-where, but codependently, we achieve great things. There is no need to desire to want to be an eye, or the head, or fingers, when God is calling you to be a mouth. When you are in place, you are happy.

Frankly, our greatest height of success or satisfaction is God's starting point. Imagine that! When God is part of your equation, the power to produce endless possibilities in the world exists. A tree doesn't produce apples just to look cute. It produces apples that humans can take and do endless things with. When I say that the possibilities are endless, I mean what God produces out of you is unimaginable. If someone can take an apple from a tree to eat, sell, do desserts with, juggle, give it as a gift, etc., how much more can God take a living person and produce never-ending fruit for the benefit of others?

PEOPLE THAT LIVED OR ARE LIVING OUT THEIR PURPOSE:

IN THE BIBLE

NAME	PURPOSE	GIFTS	PLATFORM/ ROLES
Jesus Christ	To die on the cross for the remission of the sins and salvation of mankind	Everything. All power	The Cross/ role of savior, teacher, prophet, the Messiah
Apostle Paul	To preach the Gospel to the Gentiles in different churches	Zeal, Teaching, good with words,	Churches, letter writing, prison/ Role of an apostle
John the Baptist	To pave the way for Jesus Christ	Boldness, obedience	Preacher
Mary	To birth Jesus Christ, the Messiah	Humility Courage, humility,	Mother of Jesus
Esther	To intercede for and save the Jewish nation	intercession	The inner courts of the palace

NON BIBLICAL

NAME	PURPOSE	GIFTS	PLATFORM/ ROLES
Charles Haddon Spurgeon	To be the "Prince of Preachers" and glorify God through His lifestyle	Preaching, teaching, writing, influence	Books, magazines, school to train Pastors, sermons, role of a Pastor and teacher
Mother Theresa	To be an example of God's love to the orphans at Calcutta	Compassion, humility, ability to love the unlovely	Orphanage, role of a mother to the children
Martin Luther King Jr.	To teach people how to use nonviolence to achieve justice for all	Wisdom, leadership,	Speeches, rallies, role of a preacher and teacher
YOU			

These examples lived on purpose. They didn't live for a title or money; they were sold out for a greater cause and allowed God to birth their purpose. Are you living? What is your intention in the things you do? Is it to get attention or please people or is it a genuine desire to please God? If you live a life to just please people or to get fame, it will end up in nothing. But when you chase a cause with everything inside of you because you are moved by convictions instead of recognition, you will change the world. People who don't live out their purpose are like cars that never drive, objects stuck in a box never used, food never eaten.

Is that how you want to live? No? Well get busy!

How can you get purposefully busy? Very simple. Know and understand your purpose and take inventory of your life (gifts, relationships, desires, passions). What is your vision in life? Have a vision for your life. Feel the vision. Find the vision. Follow the vision. At the end of the chapter, I have given you some exercises to help you think about this.

With knowledge and understanding, it is easier to love who you are and therefore live out what God has called you to do! Strive to be great, but most importantly, strive after what God has called you to do.

Get busy with a cause that you care about. Your most valuable asset is you and your time. Why would you waste your time doing something that is not edifying you or those around you? That is boring! You might as well go into work and sing the old Fugees song, "Killing me softly," because that's exactly what happens when we invest our time into things that are not growing us in purpose. Be smart. Get to know yourself. What your gifts are, who God is and who you are in Him. Take inventory of your relationships. Cut those that are not celebrating who you are. Nurture those that are part of your life for a reason. Embrace the pain and process in your life. Let your character be built through the hardships. Know the platforms that are in front of you to shine that light and get busy! Live! Live like today was your last day. Be aggressive in your purpose. Say yes to some of the No's in your life and just KEEP IT MOVING.

PURPOSE INGREDIENT: IN ME, BUT NOT FOR ME

The final thing you need to know as you run on your journey is that the active purpose ingredient inside of you is not for you! What we are meant to produce in life is not for us, but others. Yes, we are all here for a purpose. However, the "fruit" that comes from it belongs to God for the growth of others. Of course we benefit too, but we are simple carriers of this purpose, vessels holding a piece of God, funnels getting something put in us so we can channel it to others. Maybe God has put in you the desire to write a song. You keep hearing it in your head. The purpose of that song is to bring healing to someone's heart. You might have fear of singing or think you can't write, but all God is saying is "be obedient." Write what He gave you because someone needs to hear it. What's functioning in you is not for you. However, what's in you must be birthed through you.

When a man invests his seed into a woman a child is the result. That child is a blessing not only to the parents but to the world. If the parents serve the Lord and carry His glory, then they will instill the same principles to the children and guess what? They will keep multiplying and God will be glorified because they keep fulfilling His purpose. That's why the Bible says "be fruitful and multiply." It did not say be fruitful and then subtract, or divide or even add. No multiply! So if the parents are clueless and are making choices that curse the family, what is being multiplied? Just that.

Well, it's the same concept spiritually. God places a seed of purpose inside of us. It's an investment. We go through the process and when we birth it, He reaps the benefits because it was His seed of purpose to begin with. Look at it this way, if Bill Gates gives you 1 million dollars and tells you to multiply it, what does he expect? He expects you to go to work and multiply HIS money. He will reap the benefits because the money FIRST belonged to him. Maybe you will get a decent cut. The awesome thing about God is that He is not a greedy businessman! (and I am not saying that Gates is, but men cant be compared to God). It might be His reward, but we enjoy the blessing as well. Sometimes the very things we birth will have ripple effects for generations to come! Think of mothers who have birthed great presidents, politicians, pastors, singers, actors, musicians, and artists. Each person came through their mother, but was not created for them. They were created to serve the world through their gift. Hence the fruit of their womb will be a blessing to the person who birthed it, the people who will experience them, yet the glory will go to God. Martin Luther King, Jr., is a great example of a man who was birthed for the people. He lived out his purpose and it's still impacting nations.

Martin Luther King, Jr. was a great man, but he went through hell to bring heaven on earth. So many people want to be great, but few are willing to go through the process of birthing that greatness. If we keep in mind that what's inside of us is not ours, we humbly go through whatever it takes to get it out. Think of Mary, the mother of Christ. She was pregnant with purpose, his name was Jesus Christ. Jesus was not born for her, but for the world. His purpose was to die on the cross. He had every gift. His calling was to be our High Priest, the True Shepherd, and God's word made manifest. Mary showed us that true greatness comes from placing your life in God's hands and doing whatever He calls you to do. She accepted the task that God assigned her in spite of its difficulty, and she lived with humility and great faith, even in becoming a disciple of her son, Jesus Christ. You do not get any greater than that. Do you know what God placed in you? Let Him do it. Don't put a condom on God's potential, power, and purpose over your life. He wants to penetrate your heart and birth in you fruit that will feed the nations!

WHAT'S GREATER THAN PURPOSE?

Living with and on purpose is one of the most satisfying feelings in the world. But beyond your talents, the knowledge and understanding you acquire; beyond the relationships that will propel you in your purpose and the joy or pain that comes with it, there is one vital truth that still resonates in me: living with and on purpose must be done with an attitude of love. The question is... *how do you give love, if you feel you lack it?*

PURPOSE REFLECTION

1. In what ways are you currently utilizing your gifts and where?
2. Look at the below product. Think about how your label would look if this were a picture of you?

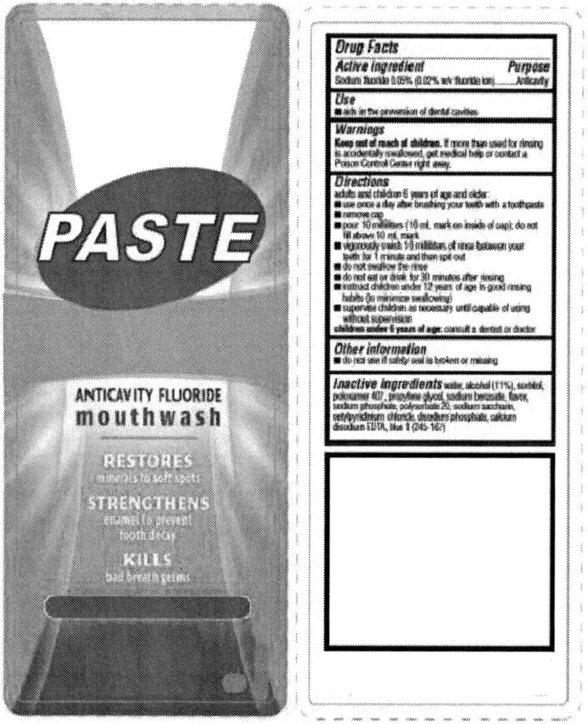

Here is what my label looks like:

ELIANA

Hebrew meaning: "My God has answered"

- A confirmed answer in your life
- Brings you understanding
- Inspires your God-esteem
- Connects you to people, purpose & God
- Loves to build people
- Networker

Life Facts

Active Ingredient — Purpose

Words — To build others with them

USE
- Communicator of Gods purpose, love and truth.

WARNINGS
- Low tolerance for intentional immaturity
- Dislikes people who are intentionally wicked.

DIRECTIONS
- Treat with love.
- Reciprocate when she communicates with you.

Other Information:

Inactive ingredients (Character flaws)
- could be intolerant sometimes
- perfectionism
- easily excuses the mistakes of others

LIVE IT TIP!

Go ahead and fill in the information you know about yourself. If you have some blanks, it's okay. As you live and discover more of yourself, fill them in. Don't rush to find some answers, rather enjoy your process, but be conscious of the different ways God

speaks to you and reveals His purpose for you.

Feel free to print this out and put it on your wall as a reminder of the active ingredient in you: Purpose.

____________________ **(YOUR NAME)** **Meaning:** **PICTURE OF YOU**	**Life Facts** Active Ingredient Purpose USE WARNINGS DIRECTIONS Other Information Inactive ingredients (some character flaws)

Appendix

Purposeful Extras

GLOSSARY

- Purpose: The reason for which anything is done, created, or exists. What something is used for. (synonyms used: Function or mission in life)

- Gifts: Spiritual and inborn God-given tools that help you fulfill your purpose.

- Talents: Physical and unique abilities that help one in fulfilling purpose.

- Calling: An inner urge or strong impulse especially one believed to be divinely inspired or an occupation, profession or career; a vocation. The position or platform you function in. (synonym used: Platform)

- Intention: The pure or impure reason or motive behind our actions. (synonyms used: motive)

- Glory: credit, fame, or honor brought to a person worthy of it.

Purpose is the different functions of God that will be carried out in you.
Calling is the position you will function in.
Gifts are tools you have been given that will facilitate the carrying out of your purpose.

PEOPLE AND ORGANIZATIONS LIVING OUT PURPOSE

Armageddon Pictures

Carlos Monroig, C.E.O

Armageddon Pictures (AP) is passionate about developing and producing inspirational, faith-based projects that are quality, entertaining, thought-provoking, sometimes gritty, with compelling stories depicting culturally relevant topics, real-life struggles and the moral challenges people face daily. Our goal is to produce projects that celebrate the importance of faith that will appeal to not only a Christian audience but a general audience as well. AP is committed to reaching out to the viewers, and is compelled to make a difference by displaying through our works, the goodness of God.

ap.productions@yahoo.com

Genuine Entertainment Group, LLC

William Morris, C.E.O and Benjamin Akuma, C.O.O

Genuine Entertainment Group, LLC (GEG) is an independent Christian entertainment company that presents authentic artists, inspirational events and overall, a genuine experience to our audiences. We seek to revolutionize the essence of Christian entertainment by exposing audiences locally and globally to a cohesive fusion of passion, quality and substance.
Genuine Entertainment Group, LLC (GEG) is living out its mission because we are making strides everyday to discover new talent and develop meaningful programming/events that will invade the hearts of our audiences.

info@genuineentgroup.com | www.genuineentgroup.com

~lglG~ let go let GOD L.L.C.
Aracely Cruz, C.E.O

The mission of ~lglG~ is to provide an outlet for believers to exude boldness. To use ones style to introduce Jesus with a smile. This clothing aims to be thought provoking and soul stirring while remaining biblically relevant. Creativity Is God given inspiration and that inspiration is being funneled through fashion to bring about salvation through The Gospel of our Lord & Savior Jesus Christ. There is no business like God's business all it takes is that mustard seed faith. Won't you plant a seed? Be Blessed & remember to let go of fear and let God work out your faith! ~lglG~

aracely.cruz@lglgdesign.com | www.lglGdesign.com

Stephanie Torres

Campus Staff Member for InterVarsity Christian Fellowship/USA

Stephanie develops Christ-centered leaders on college and university campuses. She serves the mission of InterVarsity to see students and faculty transformed, campuses renewed, and world changers developed.

ivstephanietorres7@gmail.com | donate.intervarsity.org/donate/to/stephanie_torres -- www.intervarsity.org

NUBIAN HERITAGE

Richelieu, Founder & C.E.O

Nubian Heritage has produced natural, luxurious personal care products from traditional African recipes with organic, fair trade ingredients since 1992. Today, Nubian Heritage has hundreds of natural products inspired by many cultures. The company is committed to fair trade ingredients, ancient healing philosophies, community commerce and culturally authentic treatments.

Nubian Heritage partners with global development organizations to build schools for impoverished girls in Africa, many of whom supply Shea butter and other natural ingredients.

support@NubianHeritage.com | www.NubianHeritage.com

Wavuuvi Africa

Jessica Luwandaga, President

Wavuuvi Africa is a music and missions' ministry dedicated to helping indigenous communities throughout Africa. Wavuuvi Africa aims for spiritual growth among God's people and to bring lost souls into the family of God. They strive to pass the fire of God and knowledge of his Word with effeciency while meeting the tangible needs of his people.

wisdominrhyme@gmail.com | www.wavuuviafrica.org

ACKNOWLEDGEMENTS

Dear Lord,
It was 4 years ago that you inspired this book in me and despite everything that transpired within that time, thank you for leading the way and helping me come to an understanding of my purpose in this process. Thank you for your love. You really wrote, edited, and made these words come to life! I am eternally indebted to you.

To my beautiful mother, who taught me to do everything in love and for her unconditional love towards me.
To my beautiful family (my sister Jereny Reyes, cousins, aunts and uncles), who taught me the purpose of a family and who made my early years of life so memorable.
To my TCNJ family (friends and staff), you were the first ground for me to blossom in my purpose! Thank you or believing in me and pushing me in the direction of what God was calling me to do.
To my spiritual family everywhere: brothers, sisters, and leaders, thank you for the constant prayer, encouragement and support of Gods vision in me.
To my Fantastic 3 lovely ladies (Alley, Elisa, and Noelia), thank you for allowing your friendship to be a platform for much self discovery. You have each taught me the importance of love and friendship in your own way. Divine forever.
To my dear faith boosters: Jackie Duckett, Angelika Gutierrez, and Aracely Cruz, thank you for believing in me and speaking words of

life when I wanted to give up and abort this project.
To my brother in Christ, Lawrence Alexander, thank you for teaching me the posture an author of God is to have: one of humility. Thanks for being real, blunt and supportive in the final stages of delivery!
To my brother, Tito Garcia, thank you for being obedient and giving up your time, energy, and creative gift to do the book cover. Working with you in these last months has not only increased the caffeine in my body, but it has shown me with my own eyes how a God given gift put to use, leads one to purpose.
To all the students of West New York Middle School and Memorial High school who willingly opened up to me to discuss their life and inspire me daily. Thank you. You are all valued treasure in my eyes.
To every person who is connected to me in some way, thank you for the conversations and sharing a bit of your life with me. Let's continue to inspire the world!
To all my Publication partners: You made this project possible. Thank you for providing the finances and encouraging me when I thought there was no way it would happen. I love you all dearly. Thank you!
Here are my Publication Partners:
Elisa Torres, Kelvin Hiciano, Jenderly Hiciano, Alexandra Algarin, Janely Jose, Georges Dubois, Katherine Kinard, Tonia Carr, Sharon Livingston-Allen, Jamal Ruffin, Nicholas Vargas, Morena Sanchez, and Stephanie Sanchez.
And last but not least, to the entire Godzchild Publications family and staff, thank you for being the midwives I longed for since the beginning of this project! Cheers to the first of many!

A FINAL WORD FROM GOD'S HEART TO YOURS:

Today God wants to be your purpose partner. Will you let Him? Are you willing to enter into an intimate relationship with Him, so that what is in you can be awakened and birthed? Are you willing to go through a process that will transform your life forever? If so pray this with me with all your heart:

> *Father God, I thank you for creating me for your pleasure and for your purposes. I acknowledge that I have not been receptive to your love for so long and have hid myself from your presence. Father, I believe that my purpose is hid in Christ Jesus and I believe you love me and desire to birth everything you have placed in me for your glory. I ask in the name of Jesus that you enter my heart. Impregnate me with your love, awaken the purpose in me, and give me strength to deliver your promise in me. I thank you for your gifts, purposes, and calling over my life. May they glorify you eternally. In Jesus name I pray. Amen.*

If you prayed this prayer with me Congratulations! Get ready to experience things you have never lived before. It won't be easy. There will be tough times. Sometimes labor pains will get so bad it will make you want to abort your mission. And most of the time it is uncomfortable to grow and be stretched in so many directions. BUT HOLD! It is worth it! Don't let fear stop you. Embrace your process and watch what happens. Don't worry about getting "there," but enjoy right here. God bless you and I love you.

Eliana M. Reyes

What's On Your Mind?

Just because the book is over doesn't mean our conversation has to stop. The revelations and conversations about purpose will happen daily! There is so much more to purpose. I would love to continue this conversation with you!

Feel free to email us what you thought about the book. What you liked, what inspired you? What you want to understand better? Anything! Remember purpose is a journey. You learn as you live. You live as you grow in that purpose. Let's talk.

If you want further information or simply want to continue this conversation feel free to write or email us. Also we love letters! Let us know about your purpose journey. We may publish some of your purpose stories on future projects or the website!

WRITE:

Made To Live, LLC

Attn: Eliana Reyes

P.O. Box 4161

West New York, NJ 07093

FOLLOW ON TWITTER:

@elianamreyes

VISIT:

www.made2live.net

If you would like to host a purpose party with the author or request information on Eliana's speaking, coaching and training services email us for more information at:
letstalk@made2live.net

Upcoming Books from the Made 2 Live Series

- Love: Give It

- Truth: Speak It.

- Made 2 Live: Tips and Principles for Everyday Living.

Other Books:

- Pregnant with Purpose: Reflective Workbook for Young Women

* ALL BOOKS WILL ALSO BE AVAILABLE IN SPANISH

SO I READ THIS BOOK, NOW WHAT?

Be.

Envision

Live.

Invent

Explore

Value

Experience

Incorporate faith

Now

Give Love to

Others

Do your Part, and God will do His